A Walk between the Clouds

A Walk between the Clouds

Messages from the Other Side

Patricia A. Leffingwell

iUniverse, Inc.
Bloomington

A Walk between the Clouds
Messages from the Other Side

iUniverse books may be ordered through booksellers or by contacting:
iUniverse
1663 Liberty Drive
Bloomington, IN 47403
www.iuniverse.com
1-800-Authors (1-800-288-4677)

ISBN: 978-1-4502-8097-6 (sc)
ISBN: 978-1-4502-8099-0 (dj)
ISBN: 978-1-4502-8098-3 (e)

Library of Congress Control Number: 2010918873

Printed in the United States of America

iUniverse rev. date: 1/14/11

It is with my deepest love and admiration that I dedicate this book to my mother, Annie. She was always my best friend and my source of strength. In life, she was only four feet ten inches tall; in spirit, she is a giant. She taught me that through faith and hard work anything can come true. Then and now, her message is the same—never give up on your dreams. This book is one of those dreams.

Contents

Figures and Illustrations

Foreword

"You were scheduled to die, but the universe changed." Yes, I said those words, much to my chagrin—indeed, my horror. I am trained to be a professional medium, and I currently help train student mediums. In my professional ethics class, I teach that we should never give that type of guidance. But I did. I fully expected my client, known to me at the time only as Patricia, to rush out the door screaming "turn him in" to the Cassadaga Spiritualist Camp authorities, demanding her money back, and insisting on having me kicked out of the profession!

Yes, I argued with my spirit guide, Dr. Huxley, about saying those words in a reading. He insisted, and I did. For many days afterward, I was down on myself. How could I say that? How could I explain myself? Fortunately, Patricia took the guidance calmly. She was less worried than I was and most understanding.

It was months later that she told me how it was that she came to me for a reading that fateful day. And it was seven months after the reading that the full impact of those words came to fruition.

"You were scheduled to die, but the universe changed." Thus began an odyssey for Patricia that is so perfectly documented in this book, *A Walk between the Clouds: Messages from the Other Side.*

Truthfully, her psychic experiences, spiritual encounters, dreams, visions, intuitions, and synchronicities are nothing new to me. My work and my studies since 1991 have brought me into contact with many such case histories, as well as my own experiences. But seldom have I encountered this full range of psychic and spiritual encounters by one person!

With courage and deft storytelling, Patricia enchants the reader with her other-worldly and life-changing experiences. It is a story of courage and faith. How many of us could accept "You were scheduled to die, but the universe changed" and heed that counsel seven months later?

In my considered and professional opinion, after knowing her for more than three years, Patricia is an incredible person and a first-rate storyteller. Perhaps the greatest part of all this is her willingness to share her experiences with us. This was not an easy task, given the nature of her experiences. We are indeed fortunate that the universe did (apparently) change, thus allowing Patricia Leffingwell the opportunity to still be with us and to share this amazing spiritual story.

I hope you enjoy her journey as much as I did. I'm glad the universe changed.

Rev. Don Zanghi, DMin
Cassadaga Spiritualist Camp
Cassadaga, Florida
November 2009

Note from the author: Rev. Don Zanghi, SCSCMA, is a certified medium, teacher, healer, and ordained minister. He and his wife Jeanette reside in Cassadaga, Florida. His interest in mediumship was inspired by personal experiences in Camp Lily Dale, New York, and was rekindled when he moved to Florida and began classes at the Cassadaga Spiritualist Camp.

Preface

Reality is like a ray of sunlight that is always shifting and changing. Life is seldom the way we first perceive.

"You were scheduled to die, but the universe has changed." How would you react if someone were to say this to you? Do you think you would become frightened and eventually succumb to depression? Would you panic and immediately telephone your doctor to schedule an overdue physical, or are you the type of individual who might even laugh at this prophesying statement by treating it as if it were a horrible joke?

Word for word, this was exactly what a medium said to me during a spiritual reading at the Cassadaga Spiritualist Camp, Cassadaga, Florida, in January 2007. As a high school teacher, certified in English and reading, I interpreted this statement as being past tense. I convinced myself that there was nothing to worry about, because whatever was to have happened to me had already changed. I could never have been so wrong! Seven months later, these were the exact words I remembered as I awoke in a hospital surgical intensive care unit with the realization that I had just undergone life-saving emergency brain surgery. Over a two week period, there were a total of three brain operations—operations that most people do not survive. The diagnosis was an acute subdural hematoma, or brain bleed. Oddly, I could not remember having any type of head injury that may have caused it, but nonetheless, the CAT scans proved that it was real.

Between January 2007, when Rev. Don Zanghi channeled the message via his spirit guide, Dr. Huxley, and July 18, when I collapsed, I experienced many spiritual and paranormal phenomena. There were late-night rattling doorknobs while vacationing in a historic haunted hotel, a visit from my deceased mother during my hospital stay, an electrical shock from a glowing orb, and the most mysterious of all was taking a picture of spirits while hiking in the Ozarks three days before collapsing with the hematoma. These are only a few of many such encounters during that brief time period.

There was plenty of time to think and question once I was released from the hospital. In the beginning, my curiosity pushed me to seek explanations for what I experienced during those seven months. While I did not set out to write a novel, two years of research and personal interviews resulted in the birth of *A Walk between the Clouds: Messages from the Other Side.*

If anyone were to have told me this story before my experiences, I would have been interested, to say the least, but I definitely would have remained skeptical. However, these experiences happened to me personally, and I know that what I saw, felt, and experienced was very real. I became totally passionate about researching each of these events during my three-month recuperation at home and continue seeking answers to this day. Primarily, I wanted to find out if there were other people with similar experiences, and my findings were remarkable! The universe provided me with opportunities of meeting many interesting people, each with his or her own amazing story.

My degrees are not in philosophy, physics, psychology, or theology, and therefore, I did not write this book claiming to be an expert with years of formal training and education in the sciences. I am leaving it to the experts in their fields to offer more complete, in-depth, scientific research and explanations of the spiritual and paranormal. My deepest admiration and gratitude is given to all who dedicated their lives (both past and present) searching for answers to many of the same questions that I began asking only recently.

I desperately wanted to understand all that had happened—beginning with Reverend Zanghi's message. My investigation led me into the areas of spiritualism, quantum physics, dreams and intuition, orbs, angels, ghosts, and other paranormal phenomena. I discovered that there is a spiritual synchronicity of signs and symbols that are continuously transmitting messages to us. Most of all, I learned that we each have psychic senses just under the surface waiting to be developed.

My research consisted of traditional methods of text and periodical reviews, as well as many personal interviews with professional mediums and spiritual healers. The universe also led me to many others who generously shared their own individual stories of spiritual and paranormal experiences. The following chapters are a blend of this research and my own enlightenments.

Most of the individuals, organizations, and places that you will read about have graciously given permission to use their names, while others preferred anonymity to protect their privacy. I am the photographer of all pictures included in this work unless otherwise credited.

For many years, I lived with the belief that I had a clear understanding of the unseen world of spirits. When I was actually confronted with it, I realized that there was much, much more that I needed to learn. It is my heartfelt hope that as you read the following chapters, you will learn something new and possibly even have a few of your own personal ah-ha moments.

Acknowledgments

While my name appears as the author, this book would not exist without the assistance, encouragement, and support of so many others. My lifetime on this earth has been greatly blessed, and therefore, my first thank you goes to God, the universe, and my loving angels for paving the way for me to have been surrounded by so many wonderful people.

My husband and best friend deserves special recognition. He was a wonderful nurse to me before, during, and after my surgeries; for this, I will be forever grateful. He also deserves a distinguished medal for his patience during this whole process. Writing can be a lonely profession for the author, but it can be even lonelier for the author's family. Thank you, Ralph, for your support and for never giving up on me!

To my beautiful daughters Kimberly, Kelley, and Karmon, I want you to know that I love you. You are proof positive of God's universal blessings!

A big thank you and hugs go to my longtime friends Mary Lou Sampson and Pam Bridges. You have been by my side through both the good times and the most challenging, and yet our friendships continue. Thank you for being a part of this story and a major part of my life.

I believe that we exist on Earth to learn valuable lessons, and I also believe that when the student is ready, the teacher will appear. A well known cliché—good things come in threes—proved to be true for me. First, I was blessed many years ago by having Lynn Robinson, PhD, enter my life. Thank you, Lynn, for planting those early intuitive seeds! And thank you also for the early reading of this manuscript. I know it must have been a painful procedure!

Second, Rev. Don Zanghi came into my life at a time of great change. By allowing his spirit guide to deliver a special message to me, my life changed, and I am a better person because of it. Don, thank you for your friendship and your guidance!

Third, the universe delivered medium Lydia Clar into my life, bringing with her renewed inspiration, courage, and friendship. Thank you, Lydia, for being you, and thank you for being my friend!

Early in the writing process, my friend and gifted photographer Brian Curl presented me with a spiritual picture (back cover) which he had taken near my home. This beautiful photo complemented this book by linking the magic that resides in the higher level clouds with that of the nature spirit mist at ground level. Thank you, Brian!

A large part of my journey occurred at the 1886 Crescent Hotel & Spa located in Eureka Springs, Arkansas. I wish to offer special thanks to Bill Ott, director of marketing and communications. Bill, both your review of this manuscript and the historical background information that you provided truly helped in bringing this story to life. Thank you for all of your hard work! I'm looking forward to my return trip to Eureka Springs.

My dear friend Mary Mueller volunteered her years of editing experience to read the manuscript. While the document was still in its rawest form, she painstakingly forged on. Mary, my warmest thanks and gratitude are being sent to you. You are indeed an angel.

My friends and colleagues at work were also vulnerable to my relentless requests. No one was safe! I would like to thank my buddy and partner in crime Charlda Sizemore for devoting countless hours proofreading and making those wonderful suggestions for improvements. Charlda, I will be forever thankful to you for your continuous efforts aimed at motivating me to keep going and never give up. Thank you. Great appreciation is also given to Stacy Spence and Judy Koogler for their manuscript reviews during those early days of development.

A huge dose of appreciation goes to my students during the past three years. Their excitement and interest in this project has been a great motivator for me. Many of them wanted to share their own personal stories once they understood what I went through. I love all of you, and thank you from the bottom of my heart for your support. You can finally stop asking me, "When can we get a copy of your book?"

The above list of kudos certainly does not include the names of everyone who provided permissions, background information, personal stories, artwork, and other valuable resources contained herein. The truth is that I could write another complete book with a chapter about each one of you. Please know that I love and appreciate every one of you. You are the reason *A Walk between the Clouds* has become a reality. Namaste!

Introduction

You cannot travel the path until you become the path itself.
Buddha

Do you ever wonder if you are psychic? If you have had a psychic or paranormal experience, are you comfortable sharing it with family and friends, or do you keep it secret because you are afraid they will think you are crazy? It is totally acceptable for small children to have an invisible playmate with whom they talk and laugh. Sadly, however, when an adult talks about communicating with a spirit or recounts a dream that actually came true, our culture tends to roll its judgmental eyes, creating our fears of looking foolish. This fearfulness of being laughed at is perhaps our greatest inhibitor. This book will help you become more comfortable with your psychic self and teach you ways to more fully develop your own psychic awareness.

As you travel with me through my 2007 spiritual journey in Part One and share my earlier life reflections in Part Two, allow yourself to remember similar things that may have happened in your own life. Activate your consciousness by reflecting on those experiences and then writing them down in a psychic journal. By doing this, you are granting yourself permission to set aside those fears and skepticism inhibitors. You will have taken a giant step toward developing your own natural psychic gifts.

After you have been journaling for a while, you will begin to notice distinct patterns of psychic or spiritual activities. These patterns then serve as validation that your experiences were and are very real and not a result of coincidence or your imagination. As a starting point for your journal, take an honest look at the following questions and see how many sound familiar.

- Have you ever thought about someone only minutes before receiving a telephone call from that same person?
- Have you ever been alone and heard someone distinctly call out your name?
- Did you ever take a photograph and have mysterious lights or images appear without reason?
- Did you ever wonder if you might be going crazy because you felt you were being watched, even though you knew that no one else was present?
- Have you ever felt that you were touched by someone unseen but then convinced yourself that it was your imagination?
- Have you ever visited a new place and had a déjà vu feeling that you had been there before?
- Did you ever have a dream that actually manifested and became reality?
- Have you ever met someone for the first time but felt like you have known them your whole life?

Congratulations if you answered yes to even one of these questions. Rest assured that you are not the only person having these experiences. You are among many who are now awakening to newly developed psychic sensory skills.

My guess is that you have already had some contact with the paranormal, which is why you are now reading this book. You may have had a near-death experience, or possibly an apparition has appeared to you. If so, you are not among the minority; these are actually quite common occurrences. The problem is that we have been trained to believe that such experiences are not real, and we are fearful of sharing these experiences. I was the same way before the summer of 2007. I hope that by sharing my spiritual journey and subsequent research discoveries that you will become more aware and accepting of your own psychic abilities.

I completely understand that books are read for different reasons. Some of you will focus only on my story, because something similar has either happened to you or to someone you know. Some of you may be reading it simply because of your curiosity and interest in the paranormal and will focus more on my research. While it is my hope that you will read the entire book, I have organized it into two distinct but related parts.

Part one contains the entire story of my 2007 spiritual journey.

Chapter one provides an overview of my spiritual pathway, beginning with my early childhood as I grew up with a psychic mother.

Chapter two begins with my waking in the surgical intensive care unit following my first surgery. Several unusual and unexplained phenomena happen during that time.

Chapter three time travels back to the moment when Reverend Zanghi channeled the ominous message via his spirit guide, Dr. Huxley.

Chapter four explains the history of the Cassadaga Spiritualist Camp and includes details my first orb encounters.

Chapter five describes my visit to the Arkansas Ozarks and contains historical information that validates why this part of the country has such a high spirit population. The 1886 Crescent Hotel & Spa is regarded as one of the most haunted hotels in the United States.

Chapter six documents a heightened psychic and intuitive awareness during my morning walk between the clouds.

Chapter seven opens with a story of synchronicity when I encountered a small Chinese lady in Eureka Springs, Arkansas, and concludes with my adventure into spirit photography.

Chapter eight begins with a ghost tour of the 1886 Crescent Hotel & Spa. It concludes with my brief possession while visiting my parents' cemetery in Little Rock, Arkansas.

Part two is filled with stories shared with me by others, as well as my own research, ah-ha moments, and experiences. Each chapter examines a specific element(s) contained in part one.

Chapter nine discusses the universe, energy, and life after death.

Chapter ten examines déjà vu, dreams, and intuition and is supported with definitions and examples of clairvoyance, clairaudience, clairsentience, claircognizance, and psychometry.

Chapter eleven looks at the history of spiritualism and mediums. This chapter may serve as a guide for selecting a medium.

Chapter twelve teaches about what orbs are thought to be by both skeptical scientists and by those who have had orb encounters.

Chapter thirteen reviews the history of angels and angelology. You will read excerpts from a professional reading explaining the angel, spirits, and aura colors of the front cover picture.

Chapter fourteen opens with my first ghostly encounter. You will learn about what ghosts are, what they are not, and how to protect yourself from psychic vampires.

Chapter fifteen discusses synchronicity, signs, and symbols that we encounter on a daily basis. You will learn how to recognize them and understand how they can help you live a happier and more spiritually balanced life with nature.

Whether you are new to the spiritual or paranormal worlds, an enlightened veteran, a skeptic, or somewhere in between, you are reading this book for a reason. I ask that you keep an open mind as you read the following pages, for only then will you be able to understand, as I have, that each daily experience is only a tiny part of a much greater whole. Together our thoughts, words, dreams, and actions fit together like pieces of a puzzle. This spiritual synchronicity allows each activity to unfold in the exact sequences they do.

There are no coincidences!

Part One

"There are only two ways to live your life. One is as though nothing is a miracle. The other is as though everything is a miracle."

Einstein

Chapter One

In the Beginning ...

Treasure your memories; they are seeds from which literature grows.

As a young child, I vividly remember my mother's intuitive feelings about friends or family only hours before they arrived at our front door completely unannounced. On several occasions, Dad and I watched her set extra places at the dinner table when we were not expecting guests, but by the time we sat down, we always had extra mouths to feed. At other times, she would awaken to see a bright white light surrounding a familiar face. In almost every case, the person passed away at the exact same time she saw them in the light.

These gifts were apparently shared by many on her side of the family, and I came to accept this as normal behavior for her. It was not, however, something we would talk about openly for fear of how friends and neighbors would react. This was during the late 1950s and early 1960s when psychic ability of any sort was not an acceptable practice, especially in the Bible Belt of the Deep South. I, on the other hand, had never experienced a psychic phenomenon, and I didn't want to. Then in my early twenties, I was awakened by a dear friend who appeared to me in the middle of the night. The following day, I sadly discovered that he had been killed that very night. I was not aware of it at the time, but on that night, I had received my right of passage. There was no doubt that I was my mother's daughter.

During the next several decades, I remained interested in the paranormal. Whenever the chance arose, I would read books, visit supposedly haunted houses, and sign up for ghost tours when we were vacationing. I have always enjoyed talking to others who have experienced similar phenomena or have had intuitive thoughts that they believed to come true. At the time, this was all simply a curiosity of mine. I never thought of myself as a ghost hunter, medium, fortune teller, or anything else that could be considered a psychic, prophet, or healer. It was a hobby that I enjoyed.

I had been working as a corporate advisor and business manager prior to changing careers to become a high school teacher. In early 2000, I embarked on a pathway of spiritual growth and development along with my dear friend Pam Bridges. It was also during this time when life presented me with tremendous challenges and obstacles. I now know that these challenges were building blocks preparing me for what was ahead, but at the time, I wondered from day to day how I would survive. I was in the process of making a major career change, working with my family to overcome the passing of both an aunt and an uncle, dealing with my husband's sudden stroke and his more recent open heart surgery (having now fully recovered from both), grieving the senseless murder of one of our best friends, and all the while, caring for my elderly mother as she bravely fought a lengthy illness prior to her death. We each have our own crosses to bear, and these were mine.

It is especially at times like these when we instinctively and intuitively find ways to deal with what life presents us. I initially adopted meditation as a way to reduce my everyday stresses. I quickly found this to be my safe haven; it became my escape from daily stresses and a time when I felt protected by an invisible, comforting warm blanket of love, peace, and tranquility—if even for a few minutes each day.

During those first years, I avidly became interested in ways of improving my meditation, began studying the chakras, and read anything I could find pertaining to angels and spirit guides. Pam's knowledge of past life regression, reading auras, and psychic intuition was also developing. Then, ten years ago, we visited the world-famous Cassadaga Spiritualist Camp in Cassadaga, Florida. My first reading with a medium proved to be much more than I had bargained for. He told me things about myself that absolutely no one could have known. Pam and I have continued to visit Cassadaga two or three times each year, and we always leave feeling our energy levels rejuvenated and stronger in our convictions about the pathways we have chosen. We have come to call it our "retreat."

A reading I received in January 2007, when the theme of this book actually begins, will remain with me for the rest of my life. I am not certain what I was expecting to hear as I sat down for the session, but it certainly was not, "You were scheduled to die, but the universe has changed."

Chapter Two

The Awakening

"The whole of life is but a moment of time.
It is our duty, therefore to use it, not to misuse it."
Plutarch

"You were scheduled to die, but the universe has changed." This haunting phrase continued to play in my memory as I awoke from my first surgery in July 2007. *Is it still Monday the twenty-third, or did I sleep through the night, and it's now sometime Tuesday, or possibly Wednesday? How long have I been asleep?* I wondered. As I lay there listening to the sounds and voices of the busy surgical intensive care unit (SICU), I tried to piece together the events of the past few days. I knew that I had returned to my Florida hometown, but how long I had been back and the details of exactly how I ended up in the SICU were still a bit fuzzy.

"You're awake!" announced my nurse cheerfully as she entered my room. "Can I get you anything?"

"Ice or water," I managed to whisper. When I tried to speak, it felt as if my tongue had been glued to the roof of my mouth. My throat was desert dry and scratchy. The nurse explained that they had only recently removed my breathing tube, which caused the intense, parched feeling deep in my throat.

Over the next few hours, as I drifted in and out of consciousness, I lay there listening to the rhythmic chirping of not only my monitors but those of others in the nearby rooms. I remember at times being acutely aware of the peace I felt as the calming voice repeated, "You were scheduled to die, but the universe has changed."

After what must have been several hours, my husband Ralph was allowed in for our first visit. I will never forget seeing the relieved smile on his face as he bent over to kiss me. I now know that my surgery was at 6:30 p.m., July 23, and he was allowed to see me somewhere around ten o'clock that night. It was only then, while visiting with him, that I became aware of the massive bandages covering my head. As we talked, my short-term memory began to partially return. Although it had vanished, I was able to remember the intense pain I had been suffering from a severe headache that began the morning of July 18.

I had been on vacation in Arkansas with my childhood girlfriend Mary Lou Sampson. We were born and raised there as only children, and over the years, we have become more like sisters than friends. Living four states apart has kept us from being able to visit as often as we would like to do, so a few years ago we decided to spend at least part of our summer vacations exploring our Ozark heritages and Arkansas's immense beauty together.

On this particular summer, I had flown to Little Rock on July 11. My plane arrived late in the day, following a five-hour layover at Hartsfield-Jackson Atlanta International Airport. Severe thunderstorms throughout the entire southeast had grounded or delayed most aircrafts in the region. What was to have been a five-hour trip rapidly became more than ten hours. My body was exhausted when the Delta jet finally taxied up to the arrival gate in Little Rock, and I was delighted when Mary Lou announced that we would be staying home for dinner. We enjoyed what remained of the day by relaxing at her house and had a peaceful dinner with her elderly father, who was then living with her. In many ways, he had been like a father to me, and I greatly enjoyed spending time with him. No matter how much time had passed, when we were together, it felt like time stood still. We laughed and told stories from our high school days that will never be forgotten—even though some should be erased from history completely.

The next morning, following a delightful Cracker Barrel breakfast with my Aunt Bettie, we drove first to Branson, Missouri. Two days later, we traveled the beautiful, winding back roads to Eureka Springs, Arkansas, where I encountered my first spiritual photography phenomenon. (This angelic experience will be discussed in a later chapter.) We returned to Little Rock on July 16, and the following morning I flew down to New Orleans, Louisiana, to meet my husband.

History repeated itself when I tried to leave Little Rock. Turbulent summer thunderstorms delayed my departing flight and then again postponed my connecting flight from Memphis, Tennessee. Almost two and a half hours late, I finally stepped off the plane in New Orleans. Ralph had driven to New Orleans from our home in Palm Bay, Florida, two days earlier. He was standing there waiting for me as I walked down the arrival ramp, and I remember being so happy to see him. Having lived in Mobile, Alabama, for eighteen years before relocating to Florida, New Orleans used to be an easy two-hour drive from home and had become one of our favorite vacation spots.

This was to be our first visit since Hurricane Katrina devastated the entire northern Gulf Coast the night of August 29, 2005. We had no idea what to expect once we arrived, but we were praying that our favorite places had either survived or had been rebuilt. Ralph had called ahead and made dinner reservations at Tony Angello's for that evening. Tony, the father of a longtime friend, had only recently reopened the restaurant, which had been a total loss due to Katrina's flooding. I vividly remember hearing news reports of how the Lake Pontchartrain levees had collapsed, sending the raging Mississippi River into residential neighborhoods. Everything in the area was instantly buried under the muddy and deadly water. Due to its close proximity to one of the levees, I knew then that Tony's was lost, for what I thought was forever. For this reason, I could not wait to have dinner again at one of the finest restaurants the Crescent City has to offer. Tony Angello's was back!

Our daughter Kimberly, her husband Chandler, and our grandson Conner had driven over from Mobile to spend a few days with us. They met us at the Hotel Monteleone in the French Quarter where we were all staying, and then as a family, we spent our first evening together enjoying the Italian delicacies prepared by Tony.

Over dinner I had shown everyone the digital spirit photographs that I had taken in Eureka Springs. Conner was fascinated with the pictures, and I told him stories of the ghost sightings reported in the 1886 Monteleone. As recently as March 2003, a team from the International Society for Paranormal Research made contact with more than a dozen earthbound spirits residing in the building. Conner immediately wanted to go on a ghost hunt when we returned to the hotel that evening, and I certainly did not argue with him. With his parent's permission, he and I went rambling through the halls and stairwells in search of whatever or whoever might want to make its presence known to us. Conner was so cute walking through the hallways asking, "Is anyone here? Do you want to tell us anything?" Unfortunately, we were unable to see or photograph anything that night; however, I promised Conner that I would take him on another expedition the following night.

Early the next morning, July 18, Kimberly and I met in the lobby and went for an enjoyable power walk through the French Quarter and along the levee. We meandered around Jackson Square and then strolled up and down Chartres, Royal, and Bourbon streets before making our way back to the hotel. I have always loved early morning sunrises no matter where I am, but there was an almost mystical feeling as we walked along the levee separating the Mississippi River from the historic city below it. The combination of fresh air and exercise, mixed with the highly contagious spirit of New Orleans, caused us both to feel energized and refreshed when we finally returned to the hotel.

The next item on our agenda for the day was to attend a jazz brunch at the Court of Two Sisters. This historic restaurant, another of our favorite places to dine, is located four blocks from the hotel at 613 Rue Royale. Kimberly and I agreed that we would all meet in the hotel lobby a little after eleven that morning and walk there together. There are very few visits to the Quarter when Ralph and I do not attend one of these brunches fit for a king. The area, known as Governor's Row, was the home of many early Louisiana politicians. The original resident of this building and the first to call it home was Sieur Etienne de Perier, who, in 1727, became the royal governor of colonial Louisiana. He was commissioned to permanently replace French Gov. Jean Baptiste Lemoyne, Sieur de Bienville, who had been recalled to France to face charges brought against him by his many enemies. However, Governor Perier's term in office was cut short in 1733 when Bienville returned to Louisiana and assumed his duty as Louisiana's governor.

The restaurant's name came much later when two Creole sisters, Emma and Bertha Camor, turned the building into a notions shop and supplied most of New Orleans's aristocratic women with clothing, perfume, and lace brought over from Paris. The sisters died within two months of each other in 1944. Emma was eighty-six years old, and Bertha was eighty-four at the time of their deaths. The love these two sisters shared for each other and for their home continues in present time. Many late-night guests at the restaurant have reported seeing Emma and Bertha sitting together at a table, still enjoying each other and their beloved home.

It is impossible not to feel their loving spirits or to be touched by the building's history while dining under the stately Spanish moss-draped trees in the old brick courtyard, listening to the dancing water of the fountains, and being entertained by excellent jazz musicians. And if that's not enough, all of this is happening while you are sipping mimosas and being delighted by the taste of the finest New Orleans cuisine. What's not to enjoy? Thank you, Emma and Bertha!

Following the brunch, Kimberly and I walked across the narrow Rue Royale to explore a small boutique featuring retro '60s clothing, which was making a fashion comeback. The rest of the family went back to the hotel where we were to join them in an hour or so. Almost immediately after entering the shop, I felt the pangs and early signs of a headache. Within only a few minutes, I knew I was getting an all too familiar migraine, and it was coming on quickly. The owner of the shop was burning incense, which I first thought might be aggravating my head, so I walked outside to breathe a little fresh air. Kimberly completed her purchases, and I told her that I needed to go back to the hotel, take something for my headache, and lie down for about an hour. I thought after that I would be as good as new.

Ralph was surprised when I had returned to the hotel so quickly, and I hated to tell him that I was developing a migraine. We both knew this probably meant that I would have to sleep in a darkened room while the medication took effect. But this was by no means a typical migraine. As soon as I swallowed the medication, I became violently sick to my stomach and passed out. This was before one o'clock in the afternoon, and I honestly do not remember anything until the early hours of the next morning. Ralph later told me that he had talked to me throughout the day and that I had answered him. At some point later in the afternoon when Ralph had gone to the hotel lobby to meet with Mr. Tony's son-in-law, Kimberly came to our room to check on me. She grew alarmed when she beat on our door with no response from me at all. She also said that she called the room several times but I never answered the telephone. Later Ralph wanted to see if the hotel had a doctor on call and even offered to take me to a New Orleans hospital. I apparently argued with him and adamantly declined both suggestions. Again, I do not remember any of these conversations, and I am also certain that I was completely unconscious all day in the room. *It would seem that if I were in some state of semi-consciousness that I should remember something from that afternoon, but to this day I remember nothing after returning from our brunch and becoming sick.*

The morning of Thursday, July 19, I was awake and told Ralph the only thing I wanted was to go home and see our doctor. We packed up and began driving east after saying good-byes to the family. By the time we reached Tallahassee, Florida, it was getting late, and I was feeling slightly better. We decided to check into a hotel and get some rest before continuing our trek home. When we awoke the next morning, my headache had returned, and I called our doctor. We scheduled an appointment for three o'clock that afternoon or as soon as we could get there. Following another five hours on the highway, we finally arrived. I have never been so happy to see a doctor's office!

Dr. T diagnosed me, based on what I had described to him, with a severe migraine and gave me a shot of Demerol saying, "This should knock you out for the weekend but should help." He said if I were not feeling better by Monday to call him. The shot did not help. I was miserable all weekend and at one point was about to suggest that I be taken to the emergency room. Early on Monday, July 23, Ralph called the doctor's office to tell the nurse that I was still sick and that he was bringing me back immediately. His instincts told him that time was not on our side, and he was not going to wait for an appointment. He knew that I needed help, and soon.

The doctor also suspected by this time that something other than a migraine was going on and sent me to the diagnostic lab for a computerized axial tomography (CAT) scan, which indicated that I was experiencing an acute subdural hematoma—a brain bleed. I can only remember that we went straight to the emergency room at the hospital, but I am now told that we actually went back to the doctor's office for him to read the scan, and from there, we went across the street to the hospital. Again, I remembered nothing of that last office visit—and still do not remember it to this day. I also don't remember entering the hospital. Ralph later told me that I climbed out of our Jeep and walked into the emergency room while he found a parking space. He said that by the time he had returned, I was sitting in a wheelchair and had already checked myself in, also an action that I do not remember doing.

I vaguely remembered meeting my neurosurgeon, Jonathan T. Paine, MD. *How odd to have a surgeon who is named Dr. Paine.* Now, here I was, lying in bed in the SICU and talking with my husband with an oxygen tube in my nose, wires connecting my arms to a machine that looked much like a space shuttle control panel, and tubes somewhere in the top of my half-shaven head that were creating a sound much like an aquarium filter in full operation.

You were scheduled to die, but the universe has changed.

I was moved to my own room the second day following the surgery, Wednesday, July 25, and was improving remarkably well. Then, just as quickly as it had happened in New Orleans, the headache returned. This time there was no waiting; I was rushed downstairs for another CAT scan. The bleeding had returned, and a second surgery was scheduled for the next morning, Thursday, July 26. Dr. Paine apologetically said that he had believed there was enough space between my brain and skull to accommodate any swelling, but apparently, that was not the case. They had to perform an emergency craniotomy by cutting out a piece of my skull, which would allow the brain room to swell. They would also have to evacuate the new blood that was collecting in order to relieve the pressure (i.e., the cause of my headaches). At this point, I did not care what they had to do. All I knew was that I did not want to experience the relentless torture of those headaches again. So, early on the twenty-sixth, back to surgery we went.

This time seemed easier for me than the first. I was aware of being wheeled into pre-op and was able to remember things more clearly when I awoke in the SICU. In addition to the elaborate headgear of tubes, gauze, and tape, I now also had bandages on my abdomen where they had to place the part of my skull that had been removed. Because bone is a living organism and the piece had to remain with my body, they cut me a little kangaroo pouch to hold it. And in case you are wondering, yes, there would be a third surgery to replace the bone before I could be discharged from the hospital.

The first night back in my room following that second surgery, I remember waking up during the middle of the night. I looked to my right and saw my mother sleeping in the recliner. I love her very much, and it gave me a warm, comforting feeling knowing that she was there watching over me. I almost said something to her, but she seemed to be so peaceful that I did not want to disturb her. I took a deep breath and drifted back to sleep, content just knowing that she was near. I think we never outgrow needing our mothers, especially when we are sick. My youngest daughter had been with me for a few nights following my first surgery, and now this was just like Mom to want someone to be with me around the clock.

By the way, my mother passed away November 3, 2005, nearly twenty-one months earlier. When I awoke the next morning, I looked over at the empty green recliner expecting to see her. My first thought was that I had dreamed she was there, and then I wondered if my pain medicine had caused me to hallucinate her image. "No," I spoke out loud to myself, "I saw her, and that I know for certain." She was there and just as real as I am sitting here writing this incredible story.

A few nights later I was awakened when someone took hold of my right arm. This is not at all unusual for a hospital—as anyone who has experienced a hospital stay knows. *Why do they always wait until the middle of the night to wake you up so they can give you something to sleep?*

On this particular night, I woke immediately when I felt the hands touching my right arm between my elbow and wrist. *Okay*, I thought to myself, *they're here to check my vitals and take blood*. But this was different in that the room was still dark, and the nurses always turned on the brilliant, bright ceiling lights before attending to their tasks. There were no lights in my room with the exception of a small glow from the hallway.

"Good morning," I said to the lady, although she was only a silhouette against the glowing light.

"Hello," she whispered softly.

As I became more awake, it occurred to me that these soft, warm, and obviously feminine hands were gently placed on my right arm, while my IV was on the opposite side of the bed and secured to my left arm.

"I hope you don't mind," she continued.

"Mind?" I laughingly questioned. I had been there almost two weeks, and no one had ever asked me if I would mind them doing anything.

"You are a miracle, and I just wanted to touch a miracle."

"Not at all," I said smiling at her. I have no idea how long she stayed, because I drifted back to sleep, and when I awoke, she was gone. I questioned my nurse the following morning about the identity of the gentle woman who had visited me during the night. I was quite surprised with her response.

"No one was here last night. We decided to let you get a full night's sleep, and we knew you would ring for us if you woke up and needed anything." As I laid there listening to the nurse's words, the voice began reminding me once again: *You were scheduled to die, but the universe has changed.*

Chapter Three

The Message

Embrace unanswered questions and have faith; the answers will come.

My third and final surgery was Friday, August 3. This was the procedure to replace the piece of my skull removed during the craniotomy. By this time, I was quite experienced with all of the presurgical procedures, and I definitely knew the routine! My only request was that they completely shave my head before this surgery so that my hair could grow back at the same, even rate.

As I look back on how I first entered the hospital, I can somewhat understand why only the right side of my head had been shaved—emergency surgery. I was never so surprised in my life as when I saw my reflection in a mirror following that first operation. My auburn hair was still one length and just off my shoulder on the left side, while the right side was totally bald. Instead of my hair there was a stapled, crescent incision that started from the center of my forehead, continued straight back over the crown, and then curved down and around to the top of my right ear. If this was not hideous enough, the tape used to secure the bandages wrapped around my head was securely attached to my blood-soaked hair on the left. Do I need to begin telling of the horror and pain when the tape was pulled off to change the dressing?

Following the second surgery, I convinced the nurse to cut the tape away, hair and all, as close to my scalp as possible. By this third time, everyone in the hospital knew my request was to be totally shaven prior to surgery. I do not remember them actually doing it, but when I awoke, my new, bald coiffeur was complete. All I needed was an orange robe, and I could have passed for a religious high priestess.

On Monday, August 6, I heard the magical words from my doctor, "We are going to get you out of here today." I was cautioned to make my recovery a full-time occupation and not to even think about returning to teaching for a while—a warning that I took very seriously. My doctors and nurses told me numerous times that I was considered to be their miracle patient; however, I was also very much aware that others were not so fortunate. Until this had happened to me, I was not exactly certain that I knew what a subdural hematoma was. The only times when I heard it discussed were on television shows such as *CSI*, *NCIS*, *Bones*, or *Law & Order* when the medical examiners reported their victims' causes of death.

To put it simply, the dura is the protective outer covering of the brain. A subdural hematoma is bleeding under the dura but between the dura and the brain and is usually caused by some type of trauma to the head. As far as I could remember, I had not suffered a head injury, so we were viewing my hematoma as spontaneous, which is considered to be rare. During the course of my hospital stay, I was aware of at least one man dying from this condition, while still others were entering rehabilitation hospitals in order to relearn their speech and walking skills. I felt very blessed indeed!

It was a beautiful, sunny, south Florida afternoon when Ralph at last brought me home. As we drove, I remember looking out over the Atlantic at the clear blue sky speckled only by a few tiny, puffy, white clouds. The seagulls and pelicans were dancing in the air, and everything seemed so vivid and full of life. I knew at that very moment that I would be looking at life from a much different perspective than ever before.

Mark Twain has been quoted as saying, "I have been through some terrible things in my life, some of which actually happened." This definitely would summarize my recent experiences, although not all that had happened to me was terrible; however, the events definitely could be said to be above and beyond one's normal summer vacation.

As I relaxed in the comfort of my own home, I had plenty of time to reflect, and it was then that the questions began coming.

- Had a force much higher than me actually scheduled my death and then made a change in plans?
- If I was still alive because the universe had truly changed in order for me to live, why?
- What is the universe?
- There must be a purpose for my continued life, and if so, what would that purpose be?
- Have others had similar experiences?

Brazilian poet and novelist Paulo Coelho wrote in *The Alchemist*, "And when you want something, all the universe conspires in helping you to achieve it."[1] My belief was that if the universe had placed me in this situation, then the universe would surely guide me in discovering the answers to these and other questions.

On my second day at home, Ralph assisted me outside onto our deck for some healing sunshine and fresh air. Our house is situated on the edge of a nature sanctuary, and our landscaping is thick with tropical foliage and wildlife, which includes an occasional alligator from time to time. This is Florida, after all! On this particular day, I walked to the edge of the deck and pointed down toward the water in an attempt to show Ralph a very large blue heron wading in search of food. As if on cue, a huge, bright blue dragonfly flew in and landed on my pointing finger. I stood there amazed, looking at this gorgeous creature of God as it rested from flight. "Native Americans believe dragonflies are totems which can teach us that life, like the light, bends, shifts, and adapts in various ways, making life's appearance never what it first appeared to be. According to legend, the dragonfly's magic teaches us to see beyond life's illusions so that we may find our own true vision. It calls on us to change our lives, and embrace our deeper feelings so that we will have a greater compassion for ourselves and others."[2]

Nothing like this had ever happened to me before, and I wondered why it was happening at that particular time. *Might this beautiful creature be my totem? Is it possible that it serves as a symbol of my journey in search for the truths of my own life mysteries?* The universe was speaking to me, and I knew I should be listening.

---

1 Paulo Coelho, *The Alchemist*, (New York: HarperCollins, 2005), 23.

2 Ted Andrews, *Animal Speak: The Spiritual & Magical Powers of Creatures Great & Small*. (Woodbury: Llewellyn Worldwide Ltd., 2007), 341–42.

The concept of the spiritual universe began for me on January 20, 2007, when Pam and I visited the Cassadaga Spiritualist Camp for our biannual retreat. At the conclusion of our last 2006 visit, the medium I had been seeing for many years said to me, "You really don't need me anymore. I'm always here for you if you need a validation, but you now know as much as I do. You no longer need me for readings." I remember walking away from his house wondering if I had just been given an old, medium breakup line, or if after all of my years of meditation and practice, I had finally graduated to a new level of awareness and no longer required his assistance. I was hoping the later was why he was freeing me and not that there was another reason he felt the need for us not to see each other again.

This was new territory for me. In the past, we had scheduled appointment times with our spiritual advisors in advance, but this time, I decided to let the universe guide me to the right person. Pam had an appointment prearranged with Matthew Greene, as she had for the past several readings, while I was more like a lost little puppy hoping to be adopted by the perfect family. I wandered around in the camp bookstore and kept monitoring the sign-in board where the mediums placed their names when they were available for readings, all the while checking out the books and other treasures being offered for sale. I was waiting to be inspired to make a decision. I am still not certain exactly why I ultimately chose Rev. Don Zanghi, but something pulled me toward him. I lifted the telephone and dialed. We agreed to meet at his house thirty minutes later.

I had always been so comfortable sitting with my former medium that I felt slightly uneasy as I walked past his house en route to meet with Reverend Zanghi. When I arrived, Don, as he now prefers to be called, was standing in his doorway waiting for me. We exchanged greetings, and he showed me to his upstairs office. I brought with me a recent picture of orbs that was taken during a tragic fire at my daughter's house in Atlanta. While I was in awe of the orbs in the trees near the house, Don was more impressed by the actual flame that was engulfing her home. He explained that the design of the fire, as it marched its way across the roof, had formed a Greek symbol that symbolized a new beginning. He told me that although the fire was definitely tragic, the message for her and her family was that life was about to take on a new and awakened purpose. He was so taken with the picture that I left it with him.

Don, as it would happen, channels the spirit of a doctor who, in turn, provides messages to Don's clients. Dr. Huxley was by no means shy when it came to me. In fact, I vividly remember Don sitting in front of me having an outright argument with him about something that the doctor wanted him to tell me. Their disagreement went on for quite some time, while I sat there witnessing this mortal man engaged in a dispute with a totally invisible entity. I was truly starting to wonder about my choice of mediums. *I'm sorry, Don, but that's how I felt that day.*

Finally, after what seemed an eternity, Don said rather distraughtly, "All right, I will tell her." Although unhappy about having to deliver the message, he turned to me and said, "You were scheduled to die, but the universe has changed." He proceeded to tell me that the message was so important that Dr. Huxley did not want me to leave without receiving it, and he continued by saying, "You will be able to enjoy in life what most people won't experience until after they have died."

How do you respond when hearing news like this? Exactly! I sat there and looked at him in total shock. *I was supposed to die, but the universe had changed.* We then spent a considerable amount of time discussing meditation and its importance in the healing process. He recommended that I read *A Master Guide to Meditation & Spiritual Growth* by Roy Eugene Davis and *The Power of Now* by Eckhart Tolle. I also remember him telling me that I should adopt a mantra to include in my meditation. Little did I know at the time, in only seven short months, I would be lying in a hospital bed having undergone and survived a series of major brain surgeries.

Five months later, on Friday, June 14, Pam and I traveled once again to Cassadaga. As in the past, Pam had a meeting scheduled with Matthew who was providing her with exquisite, chalk aura sketches that he had created while giving her readings. During our last meeting, he had captured a beautiful drawing of Pam's aura, and in its center was a female portrait looking very much like Pam's deceased grandmother. (Figure 3.1) Matthew told her that this was the spirit that was around her on that day.

Artwork by Matthew Greene, Medium and Spiritual Artist
Figure 3.1: Pam's Aura with Deceased Grandmother

As for me, I was still suffering from the lost puppy syndrome, and at that point, I had no ideas about where to go or who to see. I was sadly remembering that my first medium did not want me to return for whatever reason, and I was genuinely terrified to see Don again. What if the doctor of doom and gloom returned, or, even worse, what if he asked me to contact my lawyer to review my last will and testament? It is true that there are some things in life that a person just does not want to know. What a dilemma to find myself in!

Then a series of events in the bookstore happened. First, Don's name was posted at the top of the sign-in board. Second, I walked over to the schedule of events and looked at an advertisement for a past-life seminar. It was to be taught by Rev. Dr. Don Zanghi. Next, I backed away and began searching through the myriad of books when a title attracted my attention, and I picked it up. The title read: *Journey to Cassadaga: My Spiritual Awakening.* I chuckled to myself when I saw that the author was Jeanette Strack-Zanghi, Don's wife. As I stood there holding it in my hands, Pam walked up behind me and said, "You need to see this." It was the exact same book I was holding. Okay, I'm known to be stubborn, but this was a little too extreme. The universe was at work again. I made the call.

Our meeting was tense to say the least. I was not as open as I usually am during a reading, and for some reason, possibly imagined, I thought Don was also holding back. Our last meeting had thrown both of us for the proverbial loop. As I remember, neither of us discussed the doctor's message during this second meeting. Somehow, the subject of my summer plans arose, and Don immediately cautioned me to be careful in New Orleans, which was one of my July destinations. He did not want me to decide on a whim to sign up for a reading with one of the so-called sidewalk mediums. I assured him that I would not. Later, as I discussed this with Pam, we decided that it was because I had become so sensitive through meditation that it could be dangerous if I encountered any dark spirits or negative energies, even though I had long ago mastered the practice of prayer and surrounding myself with the white light of love and divine protection.

We were checked in to spend the night in the Cassadaga Hotel, and knowing that the hotel closed down at 3:00 p.m. each day, we decided to drive to nearby Orange City to pick up some sushi and wine for dinner. As we drove, I still had that haunting memory of Don's message to me.

Chapter Four

The Orb Encounters

"We are all too much inclined to walk through life with our eyes shut. There are things all around us, and right at our very feet, that we have never seen; because we have never really looked."
Alexander Graham Bell

Pam and I returned to the hotel and enjoyed our sushi as we sat outside on the porch sharing conversation with the four other guests staying on that particular night. My most spiritual moments in Cassadaga are in the late evenings while sitting in peaceful silence on the front porch of the historic hotel, breathing in the energies of the community's history.

George P. Colby (1848–1933) was the founder of Cassadaga. Colby was a trance medium and was also called the "Seer of Spiritualism."[3] He had many spirit guides, among which was a Native American named Seneca. While conducting a séance in Lake Mills, Iowa, Seneca manifested to Colby that he would establish a Southern Spiritualist Camp. In 1875, as directed by Seneca, Colby and another medium, T. D. Giddings, traveled into the wilds of central Florida before settling in what is now Cassadaga. The charter for forming the Southern Cassadaga Spiritualist Camp Meeting Association was granted in 1894. The name *Cassadaga* is derived from the language of the Seneca Indians and means "rocks beneath the water."[4]

3 *Cassadaga Spiritualist Camp: 2005/2006 Annual Program, A Brief History*, 4.
4 Ibid., 5.

I have been told that none of the original structures from those early days still remain. Most of the current buildings were built in the 1920s. The original hotel was destroyed by fire in 1926, was rebuilt, and ultimately reopened in 1928. (Figure 4.1) The Association sold the Spanish mission-style hotel in 1933, and although it is no longer a part of the camp, it stands as an anchor of the community's heritage and contains many memories and energies of bygone days.

Figure 4.1: Cassadaga Hotel, Cassadaga, Florida

The sun was setting as we completed dinner. The manager of the hotel came outside to say that he was leaving for the day, but we could make ourselves at home. He encouraged us to feel free to go anywhere in the hotel and take all the pictures we wanted. Other than Pam and I, there was a teacher from south Florida with her daughter and a young, twenty-something couple who seemed to be there more for the fun of a ghost hunt than to have a spiritual experience. *Different strokes for different folks.* The only other person at the hotel that night was the night watchman who lived upstairs in the back of the hotel. It was definitely a perfect setting for a Stephen King movie if one were so inclined.

On this particular night, Pam was staying in room number two, I was in four, the teacher with her daughter were in five, and the young couple had room number six. All of these rooms are downstairs with doors opening both to the inside hallway and outside onto the front veranda. Pam and I had been told that on the previous night a guest in room three had taken a picture of a female apparition dressed in period clothing. The apparition appeared in the mirror over the basin. The basins, or pedestal sinks, are located in the sleeping area of the rooms instead of in the bathrooms, a custom at the time the hotel was constructed. The picture generated quite a bit of excitement in the bookstore earlier that morning. We had to wonder why room three had been passed over when handing out the keys when we checked in. The teacher inquired as to whether we had ever seen anything on our previous stays, which we had not. We all agreed that it would be exciting if we were able to have an experience that night.

The hotel's ambience underwent a transformation after dark, as is true with most places. By day, the welcoming antique furniture, dark floors, and high ceilings presented a stately, old-world facade. By night, lit by only by a few, ornate, antique light fixtures, our surroundings had taken on an entirely different, other-worldly appearance. It was probably our imaginations working overtime, but as we began our photographic adventure, the entire hotel seemed to have become eerily quiet. Slowly and quietly, we began moving through the sitting area of the lobby, finally making our way to the rear of the hotel. I do not know why, but we were almost tiptoeing in the silence. We were the only people in the building, so who were we afraid of disturbing? As we stood outside the entrance of the Lost in Time restaurant, the teacher and her daughter caught up with us. We decided to stay together, at least for a while.

"Is anyone here? Say something so that we know you are here. We are your friends. Take us to your leader."

We all looked back in the direction of the lobby to see who had intruded upon our silence. None of us were terribly surprised to see that the young couple had just entered. In his right hand, he was holding something that extended upward and slightly out in front of him. A closer examination brought the realization that he was holding his cell phone and was pretending that it was an electromagnetic field (EMF) meter. EMF meters are used by professional ghost hunters to measure spirit energies when present. This guy had been watching way too much television. Pam and I exchanged glances that clearly said, "This is going to be an interesting night!" They readily joined us.

To the right of the restaurant's entrance, a stairway led upstairs to additional hotel rooms and a few offices normally occupied by mediums during the day. We took pictures from varying angles as we gingerly climbed the stairs, hesitating on the landing before continuing on to the second floor. Upon reaching the top, the young couple turned left and began walking down the long, narrow hallway, while the rest of us turned right and began flashing our cameras once again.

"Look at this. What does this look like?" Pam asked me, turning her camera around so that I could see the screen. "Is this an orb?"

"That's what it looks like!" I said excitedly.

Pam's picture was of a carpeted area in a short section of hallway, flanked on the left by one of the medium's offices and on the opposite wall by a stairwell leading downstairs into the hotel's kitchen. There, as clear as day, hovering just above the carpet was a large, translucent orb. (Figure 4.2)

Photograph by Pamela S. Bridges.
Figure 4.2: Orbs in Cassadaga Hotel Hallway

There were additional, smaller orbs to the right of the doorway about four feet above the floor. Each of them could only be seen on the digital camera screen and not with the naked eye. We had been hoping for something like this for years, and we could not have been any happier than we were at that very moment. The teacher asked to see the picture, and then both she and her daughter began snapping pictures as they attempted to also capture images of these tiny objects. By this time, the young couple overheard our excited voices and came rushing to where we were standing.

"Did you get one?" he asked.

"I got a picture of something," Pam answered.

"Come out and visit. We won't harm you," he pleaded to the spirit world, while his camera flashes were appearing more like strobe lights on a disco floor. At least by now, he had put away his cell phone (i.e., his pretend EMF sensor). He was obviously attempting to be cute to impress his companion, but his humor was beginning to irritate the rest of us. I read somewhere that if you plan to have a successful spiritual encounter, you need to leave the skeptics at home. Their negative energy can prevent spirit energy from actually manifesting. Pam and I exchanged glances with each other, both thinking the same thing. We had finally taken our first orb pictures, and we had this junior Ghost Buster wannabe with us! We did not want him to ruin our good fortune.

I was happy for Pam to have her picture, but I desperately wanted one of my own. I do not know exactly how many pictures I had actually taken, but there were a lot that I later deleted. I had taken pictures of paint spots on a couple of stairs, a few water stains, one or two dirt spots on the carpet, and many pictures of absolutely nothing. As we completed our tour of the upstairs, I took a picture of a door leading to an upstairs office and got it! There on my little camera screen was the most beautiful orb I had ever seen. It appeared to be floating halfway up the door and just inside the door frame. (Figure 4.3) Maybe I was a little biased in that thought, but nevertheless, it was tiny, it was beautiful, and it was mine!

Figure 4.3: My First Orb

Darkness had completely arrived by the time we walked out of the hotel at around eight thirty that evening. We were feeling so good about our second-floor orbs that we decided to test fate's generosity by taking a walking tour of the community. If our luck held, we might discover other energies waiting to have their pictures made. We left through the hotel's front door and turned left onto Stevens Street, which is considered by many to be Cassadaga's main thoroughfare. We were enjoying our leisurely stroll as we inhaled the sweet smell of the early summer flowers, which were in full bloom everywhere.

Cassadaga is a small community, and it does not take long to walk anywhere one elects to go. We traveled three short blocks down Stevens Street and arrived at the Colby Memorial Temple. After taking pictures of the front of the structure, we wandered around to the rear of the building. I clicked a picture of the back entrance and captured another image of a large orb that seemed to be protecting the doorway. It was located on the top right of the metal canopy above the entrance. (Figure 4.4)

Figure 4.4: Orb at Colby Temple

Pam and I were as happy as two children at Disney World that evening. Before that night, we had only read about orbs and had talked with friends and relatives who had taken pictures of these beautiful globes of energy. Now there we were with our own pictures, and we simply could not believe that we both had been so fortunate. William Shakespeare could easily have written about this in his *A Midsummer Night's Dream*, except that this was no dream, and there were no fairies. *Or were there?*

It was close to ten o'clock at night when we decided to call an end to our orb hunting. We promised to telephone each other if any spirits or other energies popped into our rooms for a visit. Cassadaga is definitely one of the most peaceful places I have ever visited. The hotel is intended for relaxation and meditation, and for this reason, there are no televisions or radios in the rooms. There is a big-screen television located in the lobby for those who simply have to feed their cable addictions, but I have never seen anyone watching it. It is wonderfully quiet.

Somewhere around ten thirty, I decided to sit outside on the porch and meditate before going to sleep. I was relaxing on a primitive wooden bench and focusing on the Eloise Page Garden directly across the street from the hotel. I happened to notice a small, round object that appeared just to the top and right side of my head. I remained very still for a minute or two, while giving some thought as to what this might be. It looked like an orb, and we had photographed them enough times that evening that I knew what they looked like. However, the orbs we photographed could not be seen by the naked eye. This orb not only could be seen, but it seemed to be hovering in space and watching me.

It must be a spot on the lens of my glasses, I thought to myself. I rationalized that if I turned my head to the left, then it would seem that the spot should move with me. I turned my head; the spot did not move. If anything, it grew slightly larger. *Okay, Patricia, we definitely have a situation here.*

This was one of those moments when I needed either my Kodak or my cell phone camera to document what was happening. My cell phone would also have allowed me to call Pam and have her step outside and witness this. Unfortunately, I had neither. I was afraid that if I went inside my room to retrieve the camera, whoever or whatever was there would leave. So I just sat there. I am not totally certain of how long I (we) remained there observing each other, but it seemed like forever. In actuality, it was probably more like three to five minutes. I could see that it was not solid, and it had both transparent areas and solid sections. Its diameter was four to six inches, but it was not perfectly round. Its edges looked soft and cotton-like, and it appeared to be fluctuating in both shape and size. As for the color, I would say that it was predominately a yellowish white, but the porch light was one of the yellow bug lights, which could have altered its color.

As I sat there looking at this miraculous entity, I not only felt comfortable in its presence, but I instinctively knew that there was intelligence contained within its sphere. However, my next move created one of those times when you ask yourself, *What were you thinking?* It also convinced me that this ball of light was much wiser than yours truly. I have always been a curious person, and like the curious cat, I usually cannot leave well enough alone.

It could not have been more than a foot away from my forehead and only a couple of inches above my head. I silently asked, *I wonder if I can touch it.* Please note that the operative word here was *can.* I didn't ask myself should I touch it, or would it be bad for either of us if I touch it? I simply wondered if I could physically reach out, touch it, and see for myself what it felt like. Would it be soft, firm, hot, or cold? Would I be able to feel anything at all? Was I really seeing what I thought I was looking at?

Without waiting for an intelligent answer from myself or the universe, I proceeded to gently raise my right arm. I slightly extended my hand at an even height with the orb but just out to its right side. You might say that the location of my hand was at about three o'clock, and the orb was at one o'clock. Without giving further thought, I began to move my hand from right to left. At the exact moment I reached the orb, my entire arm jerked back from what felt like a mild electrical shock. It was not painful, but I definitely felt that I had moved through an energy field of some sort. I felt a mild tingle straight up through my fingers, and it continued up my arm, to my neck, through the right side of my face, and up into my head. It was only at this very moment that I questioned my common sense and spoke out loud. "What were you thinking? Maybe you should not have done that!"

With that one simple wave of my hand, the orb was gone. I did not know if I had frightened it away or if I had injured it by passing through its energy field. I had only read about what orbs are thought to be. I have never studied what happens if you actually touch one, and I definitely had done that. I made a mental note to find information about the effects of orb energy on humans. Better late than never!

Before I went back to my room, I glanced down the porch toward Pam's room, hoping to see a light. I really wanted to tell her about this incredible encounter. There were no visible lights, so I went inside and attempted to go to sleep. I had just curled up in bed and turned off the lamp when I noticed something on the ceiling. I lay there staring at this white circle that was just to the right of the ceiling fan. My heart was racing with excitement, and I was convinced that I was looking at another orb. I rolled over in the darkened room, grabbed my camera from the night table, and snapped three frames in a row before I turned on the light. I laughed out loud as I examined my newest images. I had taken award-winning pictures of the rare and elusive smoke detector. This was yet one more example of the dragonfly lesson—things are not always as they appear.

Early on Saturday morning, June 15, Pam and I were anxious to talk to the experts in the bookstore about what we had seen and experienced. We entered the charming little shop as soon as the doors were unlocked and found the workers smudging with sage to eliminate negative energies from the previous day. The girl working behind the counter asked us if anything unusual had taken place. We began sharing our orb sightings and telling of the pictures we had taken. I decided to remain quiet about my smoke detector pictures.

As the early morning visitors began entering the bookstore, I happened to catch a glimpse of a familiar face near the front door. Reverend Zanghi had arrived and was walking toward the sign-in board. My first reaction was to somehow slip away without being seen, but at the same time, I was pulled to talk to him. I moved to a counter nearer to him and began asking the clerk about a statue of Buddha located on a top shelf. This was a particular Buddha, sitting in the lotus position, that I had been searching for over the past couple of years. It was hand carved from a lightweight wood, about twelve inches in height, and hand painted in black with gold trim—and it just happened to be within my price range. As I completed the purchase and turned around, I noticed Don standing only a few feet away.

I spoke first, "Hello."

"Good morning. How are you?" he asked.

"I'm wonderful. I saw and actually touched an orb last night," I exclaimed sounding like a child announcing seeing the tooth fairy.

He looked at me inquisitively. "So you felt the energy?"

"I certainly did!" I halfway expected him to question me about it, but in his profession, I guessed that he already knew what the energy feels like. Longtime Spiritualists do not seem to have the same enthusiasm as us first-time orb photographers. They have seen hundreds and thousands of orbs during their careers.

I sensed he had something he wanted to say as we stood there looking at each other, exchanging silence in lieu of words. Don finally spoke, "I wanted to come and find you yesterday after you left."

"Oh?" I responded curiously.

"In fact, I would have, except my wife and I had some important shopping to do, and we were gone for most of the day. The entire time we were away, I kept telling her that I really should have talked to you about our last meeting. I have never in my life told anyone that they were scheduled to die. This has troubled me ever since I said it. In all the years I have been counseling, I have never said anything like that. I mean, to tell someone they were going to die …"

I then understood my intuition about yesterday's reading. Don had been as tense as I was, and for all the same reasons.

"I didn't know how it might have affected you," he continued. "For some people, it might have sent them into a depression—anything could have happened. You never know how someone might react when they are told something like that." It was easy to see and feel his genuine concern.

I assured him that although I never forgot, not even for one minute, what had been said, it certainly was not something that could have caused me to have a nervous breakdown, or worse. I mean, after all, the message was *the universe has changed*, right? For me, that phrase was past tense and not something that was lurking in the future. What did I have to worry about?

We talked for a while longer, and he looked at my Buddha, suggesting that I place it somewhere high so that it would be looking out over our living area, which was exactly where I had planned to place it. The Buddha's purpose was to be a symbol of continued peace and harmony for our home. We parted amicably and promised that we would stay in touch with each other. Don gave me his business card and asked me to let him know if he could ever do anything to help. I felt much better about my new friend as Pam and I said farewell to Cassadaga and began our journey home.

We chattered enthusiastically for the entire two-hour drive. Pam had received her third aura sketch by Matthew, and this time the spirit energy appeared to be her late grandfather. We both had taken some excellent orb photographs, and I was feeling much happier about my most recent conversation with Reverend Zanghi. I cannot remember even thinking one time about the doctor's message for me.

Our orb experiences had been so wonderful that I was now even more excited about meeting Mary Lou in Arkansas in less than a month. Our reservations were at one of America's most haunted hotels, and I found myself hoping that I might be able to photograph other orbs. Would it be possible to have two such experiences in one summer?

Chapter Five

Spirits in the Ozarks

"... a cloud was coming down as we 'rose ...
then I was alone on this cloud ... and I was no longer afraid.
I knew I was going home."[5]

Black Elk

I flew to Little Rock, Arkansas, on July 11 to meet my girlfriend Mary Lou. We had grown up in North Little Rock and had recently made the decision to spend part of our summer vacations exploring our Ozark heritage. Early on July 12, we visited with my Aunt Bettie before driving to Branson, Missouri, for the first stop of our Ozark expedition.

What a laid-back and grandiose place to be! We enjoyed two glorious days in booming Branson, which had been exactly what the two of us, being long-time high school friends, had needed to rekindle the fun and innocence of our bygone days. Although there was much to see and do, the highlight was when we went to Dick Clark's American Bandstand Theater. Our hotel concierge assisted us in getting tickets to the Original Stars of American Bandstand performance, and for two solid hours, we were entertained by music we enjoyed as high school students in the 1960s. We listened to nonstop hits performed by artists Fabian, Bobby Vee, Brian Hyland, The Chiffons, and

5 John G. Neihardt, *Black Elk Speaks* (Lincoln: University of Nebraska Press, 1988), 226.

Chris Montez. We were so hyper when we returned to the hotel that we stayed up most of the night laughing and sharing high school memories.

It was midmorning, Saturday, July 14, as we bid farewell to Branson and set our sights on Eureka Springs, Arkansas. Our plan was to take a back roads driving tour, and we were very glad we did. The scenery was magnificent! I wish now that I had actually counted the deer that either crossed the road in front of us or simply stood on the side of the highway and watched us pass by. At times, it felt as if they were welcoming us into their secret, magical, mountain resort.

As we traveled the meandering, tree-lined, mountain roads, I was awestruck by the foliage and clarity of the air. At one location, I asked Mary Lou to pull over and stop so that I could take pictures. We had somehow driven down through a layer of clouds and were now in the midst of an open space. The magnificence of the Ozarks spread out both above and below us in all its grandeur and splendid beauty. We parked on a wide, grassy shoulder of the road where we looked out at another mountain rising up across a deep, rich, green valley. Another layer of clouds blanketed the earth below. We were actually between the clouds, and the view was breathtaking. I recalled an old saying that I heard as a small girl: it's not that the Arkansas Mountains are so high; it's just that the valleys are so deep. At that specific moment, I understood its true meaning, and I remember thinking that I wanted to stay right there and never leave.

We watched as an eagle soared first above us and then out over the valley before disappearing. I felt quite small as I stood watching the great bird floating downward into the clouds below, vanishing before our eyes. There were neither sounds of the hustle and bustle of a city nor noise of people rushing to get to work or hurrying to return home. I wondered if this might be what heaven is like. I also considered that we might never have this experience again once we left that particular spot and it saddened me to walk back to the car to leave. This was a one-act play presented by our Earth Mother, and we had front-row seats. I so loved this extreme beauty, and I felt at peace with the world.

We arrived in Eureka Springs slightly past noon. Almost on cue, another deer darted across Highway 62 in front of us just as we passed the city limits sign. We followed the signs from Historic Loop (Old 62B) and began our ascent up Crescent Drive toward our ultimate destination of the 1886 Crescent Hotel and Spa located on the north crest of Crescent Mountain. The road led us upward from Highway 62 and through the historic town, all the while wrapping its way up the side of the mountain.

As we passed through the town, we were completely captivated by the picturesque, pastel-colored, Victorian-style homes nestled among the trees. The view was spectacular as we drove still higher and higher. The road was surrounded by towering trees allowing through only streaks of filtered sunlight, creating a soothing and welcoming glow over us. I could feel my pulse rate increasing with excited anticipation with each turn we made. This was proving to be even more wondrous than I had ever imagined. As we neared the summit of the mountain, we passed by beautiful St. Elizabeth Catholic Church on the right, and as I looked up to the left side, I was able to see our hotel located one tier above. The towering magnesium limestone structure, in all its Victorian-French-Gothic glory, appeared as the crown jewel for this mountain retreat. (Figure 5.1) My heart skipped a beat! This was magnificent.

I do not think I will ever forget driving into the parking lot in front of the hotel, stepping out of the car, walking past the huge fountain topped by a brass crescent moon, and finally entering the lobby of this Grand Old Lady of the Ozarks. The hotel first opened her welcoming arms to greet guests during its grand opening on May 20, 1886, slightly more than one hundred twenty-one years earlier. Now, here we were stepping back into history, if only for two short days. The energies of the past were the first to greet us with a warm welcome, and we were both instantly enveloped with the soothing comfort of finally being at home.

Printed with permission of the 1886 Crescent Hotel & Spa
Figure 5.1 Historic Image of the 1886 Crescent Hotel & Spa

Earlier in the year when we were formulating plans for this trip, Mary Lou had mentioned several potential locations, including my birthplace of Hot Springs. I was unaware of it at the time, but the universe had spoken to me again. Mary Lou had only to mention Eureka Springs and the Crescent Hotel, and chills ran up and down my arms. I knew instantly that this would be our ultimate vacation, even though, at the time, I knew absolutely nothing about the area or why I felt so strongly about going there.

My reaction did not surprise my friend. She laughingly said, "I knew that would be your choice."

"Why would you say that?" I questioned.

"The Crescent Hotel is haunted. I thought you knew that."

"No, I didn't know," I said inquisitively.

"The hotel was featured on the Syfy Channel's *Ghost Hunters* program as one of America's most haunted hotels. The Atlantic Paranormal Society (TAPS) investigated the hotel a couple of years ago and proved that there is paranormal activity. They saw a full body apparition in what used to be the morgue."

"You're kidding! I really didn't know anything about it being haunted." She definitely had my attention, and after a couple of minutes of thoughtful silence, I asked, "The hotel has a morgue? Hmmm!"

"The *Ghost Hunters* team used a thermal imaging camera in their investigation of the hotel. When they showed the picture on television, they called it "the holy grail of ghost hunting." I knew you'd want to go there, but I thought you already knew the hotel is allegedly haunted."

This new information was music to my paranormal ears, but knowing that Mary Lou did not exactly share my passion for the spirit world, I asked, "Are you okay with staying there?"

I could hear the reservation in her voice when she replied, "I think so." She then giggled a slightly nervous laugh and said, "At the least, it should be an interesting trip."

A past-life medium once told me that I am an ancient soul, and I now wondered if somewhere in my spiritual family tree I had ever lived there before. That could definitely explain why I felt so strongly about visiting there. During the next few months, I would discover that the hotel, frequently called The Grand Old Lady, had already lived a full and diverse lifetime. Had our paths crossed before?

My curiosity has always demanded that I educate myself about a new destination before actually going there. Almost immediately after Mary

Lou's telephone call, I began compiling a list of topics to research before our Ozark pilgrimage.

- What was the history of the area?
- Why would this hotel and town tend to have more spirits than any other?
- What would make someone want to invest in a building project of this magnitude in such an out-of-the-way place as this small Ozark hamlet in the 1880s?
- What did it have to offer during the post Civil War era?

Archeologists have documented that the first Native Americans in Arkansas inhabited the Ozark Mountains during the Paleo-Indian period, 13,500 years ago. This would date them to 11,500 BC, the end of the ice age and when the first traces of North American humans appeared in archaeological records. These early Arkansans lived in overhanging cliffs and caves throughout the Ozarks. Partly mummified bodies of these rock shelter people, wrapped in hemp blankets and robes of feathers, have been uncovered only twelve miles west of Eureka Springs. *These historical facts validated a centuries old potential for spirit energies in this geographic area. This was a big ah-ha moment for me and I hadn't even begun to review Arkansas's Civil War and more modern history.*

The next known inhabitants were the Osage Indians dating back to the mid to late 1700s. The Osage believed the mountain springs near the White River, which they called Blue Spring, contained magical healing powers, and they referred to the area around them as sacred ground. Between the fall of 1838 and the brutally fierce winter of 1839, the Cherokee people adopted Blue Spring as a renewal site along what would become known today as the Trail of Tears. These great and proud people had been stripped of their rights and dignity, physically removed from their homelands east of the Mississippi River as an action of the 1830 Indian Removal Act, and forced to relocate to reservations in Oklahoma.

It is said that at least four thousand Cherokee died during this voyage, giving way for the Cherokee name "Nunna daul Isunyi,"[6] meaning "The

6 Reynolds, David S. *Waking Giant: America in the Age of Jackson*. (New York: HarperCollins), 316.

Trail Where We Cried." Although these tribes oftentimes battled, they shared the waters of Blue Spring in peace, because it was the Great Spirit's sacred ground. Legend has also been passed down that Florida Native Americans told early explorers stories of magical healing waters, and that Blue Spring was actually Ponce de Leon's fountain of youth. This mystery remains unresolved to this day. *These tragic Trail of Tears deaths added another layer of documentation to my earlier evidence. The Ozark Mountains definitely had the historical elements necessary for a large spiritual population.*

Dr. Alvah Jackson was the first white man of record to discover these healing springs. Circa 1854, he and his twelve-year-old son had been hunting when his son injured his eye. The doctor washed his son's inflamed eye in the crystal water of what is now known as Basin Spring, and within a couple of days, the boy's eye had healed. Basin Spring is located in the center of what is now Eureka Springs. The doctor successfully marketed the water as Dr. Jackson's Eye Water, and soon the entire area soon became widely known as Indian Healing Spring.

A few years later the Civil War had broken out, and fighting found its way to this tranquil setting. Dr. Jackson built a primitive hospital inside a cave near the springs. As with the earlier Native American tribes, both Union and Confederate soldiers peacefully shared the hospital and healing springs of the sacred ground. *Hmmm? The* Ghost Hunters *team captured the image of a confederate solider. Is this just a coincidence?*

The war ended in 1865, and by the late 1870s, life in the United States had returned to normal. Wealthier families were traveling to resorts famous for their healing qualities of the natural waters. The bustling little settlement had by then grown to some five hundred homes, and on July 4, 1879, its name was officially changed to Eureka Springs. At the same time, an outbreak of yellow fever broke out in Memphis, Tennessee, and in the Mississippi Valley of Arkansas. Stories of the magical healing springs brought even more people to the area, and by the early summer of 1880, the population had grown to fifteen thousand people. *Interesting! Many people died here during this epidemic, adding to the spiritual evidence.*

The hotel began as a dream of the Eureka Improvement Company (1880) under the direction of a former governor and Civil War general, Powell C. Clayton (1833–1914). Isaac S. Taylor of St. Louis was commissioned as the leading architect of what would become a castle towering over the mountainside village of Eureka Springs. When completed, it would not only be the town's first stone structure but would also become "America's most luxurious resort hotel."[7]

I had now answered my question as to why a group would be willing to invest $294,000 in 1880 dollars to build a five-story hotel on the top of this remote, crescent-shaped mountain. The answer was now clear—capitalization and modernization had at last arrived in the Ozark Mountains.

The Grand Old Lady did not always embrace peace and prosperity. The depression era of the 1930s also created a dark period in the history of Eureka Springs and for the Crescent Hotel. By 1934, the hotel had closed its doors due to lack of paying guests and sat empty until 1937 when Dr. Norman Baker purchased the hotel and created the Baker Hospital and Health Resort. The doctor, who claimed to have a cure for cancer, said that he was relocating patients from his privately owned Baker Institute in Muscatine, Iowa. What he did not make completely public was that he had been run out of his home state of Iowa for practicing medicine without a license, among other charges. He, in fact, was not a doctor at all. Dr. Baker, a high school dropout, was a former machinist, vaudevillian, inventor, radio broadcaster, and self-proclaimed physician.

It is said that Baker used this new location to secretly experiment on his patients while he was hoping to actually find a cure for cancer. While he claimed to cure patients without surgery, he actually tortured them with injections of a secret formula. This formula was a solution made of watermelon seed, corn silk, clover leaves, alcohol, carbolic acid, and glycerin.

Under his direction, many of the patients went insane with the treatments, and hundreds of others died between 1937 and 1939. Affluent families paid to have their deceased sent home for burials. Tragically, others who were not so fortunate were carried to the basement on gurneys during the night and burned in the incinerators. Sadly, I have been told there still remain many patients whose bodies have never been accounted for. It is believed that they may be buried somewhere on the side of the mountain. *These tragic deaths certainly add to my growing list of reasons for the existence of lost spirits in this area.*

In January 1940, a Little Rock Federal Court tried and convicted Baker for federal mail fraud due to his promises of curing cancer. While he had defrauded $4 million from cancer patients, he was only sentenced to four years in Leavenworth Federal Penitentiary and fined $4,000. Following

---

7 *Welcome to the Historic 1886 Crescent Hotel & Spa. Crescent Hotel Opens Today:* Brochure reprint from May 20, 1886 edition of the Eureka Springs Times-Echo, 2007.

his release, Baker lived in Dade County, Florida, until his death in 1958. Today, many claim to have seen Dr. Baker's ghost walking through the hallways of the Crescent.

Ghost stories of apparitions, spirits, manifestations, and legends abound in the hotel and surrounding town. The earliest story for the hotel dates back to its construction in 1885. An Irish stone worker, known only as Michael, fell to his death from the roof into what is now the location of room 218. Workers in the hotel, as well as guests, claim that Michael opens and closes doors, moves items in the room, and oftentimes his screams can be heard from above the room's ceiling.

My research definitely revealed the potential for a very large population within the spirit community. I was, however, still wondering why I felt such an intense need to be there. What was the universe trying to tell me?

Chapter Six

Angels, Spirits, and Ghosts

"... And while I stood there, I saw more than I can tell,
and I understood more than I saw;
for I was seeing in a sacred manner the shapes of things in the spirit, and the shape of all shapes as they must live together like one being ..."[8]

Black Elk

We felt as though we had stepped into a time machine and had somehow been transported back to 1886 as we stood at the majestic antique registration desk. Everything about the lobby had been restored to appear exactly as it had one hundred twenty-one years earlier. I felt as though I had left my mark in history when I officially signed the oversized, leather-bound guest book. As we were talking with the bellman about our luggage, and as if on cue, a horse and carriage arrived at the front entrance to pick up some lucky passengers. This was definitely a slice of heaven.

Our room was a comfortably decorated room on the fourth floor with a bird's eye view of the east lawn, the site of many wedding ceremonies. In fact, this romantic setting was host to at least five weddings during our two-day visit. After unpacking a few things, we went downstairs for a relaxing lunch in the Crystal Dining Room Restaurant before catching the trolley for a downtown excursion.

8 Neihardt, 43.

Our trolley driver, having been a lifelong resident of Eureka Springs, was very knowledgeable of the town's history. We had already noticed the unusual winding streets when we first arrived, and he explained that *Believe It Or Not!* ®had featured the town as being the most unusual in the United States because of its street design. (Figure 6.1)

Printed with permission of Ripley Entertainment, Inc.
Copyright notice © 2007; Believe It or Not! ®
Figure 6.1: Robert L. Ripley's 1930 Illustration of Winding Streets in Eureka Springs, Arkansas

Our guide told us that the Native Americans and animals first designed the unusual mapping of the streets. The steep slope of the mountainside dictated that they follow pathways of least resistance, and the design stuck. Mr. Ripley described it as "a town with winding streets without a single street crossing or stop light." As the buildings were constructed, they also followed the lay of the land. Many of the home sites were literally blasted out of the limestone rock and were laid out in stories up and down the hillside. "It's not unusual," our guide continued, "for a building or home to have multiple addresses." The 1905 Basin Park Hotel for example, also described by Bob Ripley, is the only hotel in the world to have eight stories, with each at ground level on different streets. (Figure 6.2)

Printed with permission of Ripley Entertainment, Inc.

Figure 6.2: Robert L. Ripley's 1930 illustration of the 1905 Basin Park Hotel, Eureka Springs, Arkansas

As we made our way into the historic area, he quickly pointed out bullet holes in the side of a stone building. He told us that they were made during what is now referred to as the Great Eureka Springs Bank Robbery of 1922. The city made national news when five men from Oklahoma made an ill-fated decision that the First National Bank of Eureka Springs was an easy mark for quick cash. The would-be bank robbers had a plan that turned out to be a chain of bad mistakes. Their assumption was that Eureka Springs was a sleepy little mountain town, making it easy prey for their unlawful greed. Having staked out the town every day for a week, it was determined that the majority of the town's employees went home for lunch at exactly twelve noon. This would leave one woman working alone in the bank during the lunch break. The crooks planned to take full advantage of this situation by arriving at the bank at exactly 12:05 p.m., making quick work of the heist, and then speeding away in their Model T automobile before any of the townspeople knew what had happened.

Like clockwork, the quintet arrived at the bank at exactly 12:05 p.m. on Wednesday, September 27, 1922. While twenty-one-year-old Mark Hendricks kept the getaway Model T touring car in readiness, Charles and George Price, Cy Wilson, and John Cowan entered the bank. The gang noticed customers completing their transactions and waited for them to leave before raising their pistols and demanding, "Stick 'em up.... All of you!" Not one of the foursome noticed the bank clock, which read 11:05 a.m. They had arrived one hour early, a mistake which would prove to be their undoing. Cashier Tobe Smith raised his hands slowly as he tapped the silent alarm heard in three different locations outside the bank.

It has been described that the next ten minutes would be reminiscent of an old west shoot-out in Dodge City or Tombstone. Business owners came to the defense of their townsmen fully armed with pistols and shotguns. By the time the smoke had cleared, Cy Wilson was lying dead on the blood-soaked Spring Street cobblestones. John Cowan was downed at the top of a stone staircase with his hip and foot severely wounded. George Price died from gunshots to the head twenty minutes after being transported to the hospital. His brother Charles died four days later from extensive internal injuries. Hendricks and Cowan survived their gunshots and received prison sentences one year later. It is unknown why they arrived at the bank one hour early, but it is speculated that as the gang sat around a campfire the night before, Charles Price inadvertently moved the hand back one hour as he was winding his timepiece. This was a very costly mistake indeed.

It is believed that in some cases where sudden or tragic deaths occur, souls might not cross over into the light either because they do not know they have died, or they have unfinished business. I found myself wondering if anyone had ever reported encounters with residual spirits from this outlaw gang.

The trolley dropped us off at the base of the mountain in the heart of the historic district. We crossed the street and climbed up two high stone steps leading from the street to an elevated sidewalk, a custom when the town was built so that women would not soil their dresses from the dirt and mud of the roadway. We noticed Basin Spring Park where people were gathering to watch some type of show. Drums began playing a rhythmic chant while a young girl in her twenties began dancing with fiery torches. (Figure 6.3)

Figure 6.3 Dancer and Drums in Basin Spring Park, Eureka Springs, Arkansas (*Faces blurred to protect identities.)*

As she danced, the drumming became more and more intense. Mary Lou was excitedly watching, while my own heart was pounding.

"Isn't this exciting?" asked my smiling friend.

"Oh, it's exciting all right," I replied rather sarcastically.

"Are you okay?" she asked, noticing my obvious nervousness.

"It's this music. It's giving me the creeps."

"Why? It's different. I kind of like it," she said happily.

"Lou, it reminds me too much of a black voodoo that I once heard in New Orleans." I was beginning to have problems breathing due to a tightening in my chest. With each beat of the drums, my breathing became more aggravated. While I recognize and appreciate that voodoo is a religion, I also know there are groups that practice a black voodoo. For me, this music definitely sounded dark, and I had to get away quickly.

"You can stay here and watch for a while if you want. I'll meet you in that little gift shop." I was pointing to a small shop between the park and the Basin Park Hotel.

"Are you sure you're okay?"

"I will be, but I can't stay here right now." As I walked hurriedly away, I noticed from the corner of my eye that the dancing girl had caught her pants on fire while passing the torch under her leg. The drums began beating faster as she patted the flame out with a jacket or heavy sweater. The crowd cheered, and she continued her chilling dance. I immediately began a walking meditation as I called upon God and Archangel Michael to protect me with the white light of love and divine protection. Almost instantly, I felt much calmer and at peace once again. I would later discover that Basin Spring Park hosts a variety of entertainers and music throughout the year. At any given time, one can enjoy bluegrass, gospel, country and western, rock, folk, big band, etc. Eureka Springs is very proud of its Free Music in Basin Spring Park and rightly should be.

Following a delightful dinner outside on the upper balcony of the Basin Park Hotel's Balcony Restaurant, Mary Lou and I made our way back up the mountain to our castle in the sky as the sun slipped behind the mountain. Darkness falls more rapidly in mountain valleys, and this was a new moon night, which would make the night appear even darker. On the way to our room, we made a quick stop at the ghost tour registration office, located on the third floor, and signed up for the following evening. While my friend had agreed to the tour as a humoring gesture to my curiosity, I could tell she was apprehensive in saying yes when I suggested it. The tour would be in our hotel, so she felt that if things got to be too much for her, she could easily leave and go back upstairs to our room. I continued to assure her that she would be safe, but I am not certain that she actually believed it.

Mary Lou jumped into her bed and went to sleep almost as soon as we entered the room. I turned on the television for a short time before I became wide awake and hyperactive. For about thirty minutes I unsuccessfully tried to relax. My adventuresome curiosity was working overtime again and was urging me to go exploring. I woke Mary Lou briefly to tell her where I was going, grabbed my camera, and slipped out into the hallway.

I had not noticed it when we first checked in, but the lounge area just outside our room was named for Dr. Norman Baker. I remember being told by our bellman that this area had at one time been used as the nursery and children's wing during the Baker Hospital era. A chill breezed across me as I stood looking down the long, narrow hallway. I wondered silently, *Are there spirits of young children trapped and standing somewhere nearby? If so, are they the young cancer patients who died so violently under Dr. Baker's care?* Again, chill bumps appeared on my arms.

I wandered through the hallways and up and down the stairways taking numerous random pictures. To my delight, I was able to capture two single orbs on two different stairway landings. I made a mental note to call Pam the next day and share my good fortune. Before returning to our room, I sat for a while in a white wicker rocking chair on the back veranda and meditated while giving thanks for the opportunity to experience this hotel and the sacred ground of the Great Spirit. A small gray cat exited the hotel through a pet door leading from the lobby onto the veranda and rubbed against my leg. I then remembered a granite tombstone marker located just below where I was sitting. The inscription read "In Loving Memory of Morris." It was the burial site of a stray cat that had become a mascot of the hotel. (Figure 6.4) Morris called the Crescent home for twenty-one years before his death on October 24, 1994. I especially liked it that the Crescent is a pet-friendly hotel allowing guests to bring their pets as long as they are properly supervised.

Figure 6.4 In Loving Memory of Morris. 1886 Crescent Hotel & Spa, Eureka Springs, Arkansas, July 2007.

Looking at this small gray feline who had now joined me, I wondered how many stories it might tell me of the spirits residing here. As with small children, animals have uninhibited senses that allow them to see, hear, and feel spirits that most humans cannot. Following about ten minutes of petting him and listening to his roaring purr, I bid goodnight to my furry little friend and went back to our room for some much needed sleep.

A rattling of our doorknob awakened me at around three o'clock in the morning. I remained in bed listening to see if it would happen again. Within a few minutes, it rattled a second time. It sounded as though someone was standing just outside our room playing with the knob but not actually trying to open the door. I wondered if someone had returned to the hotel late and was trying to enter our room by mistake. The facts were that it was three fifteen in the morning, there had been several weddings in the hotel that day, and there had been a lot of liquid spirits consumed. It would, therefore, make perfect sense for someone to come upstairs late and be confused about rooms. However, whoever was outside our door did not have a key. This sounded more like something a child would do if running and playing in the hallway, randomly grabbing at the knobs as he passed. I slid out of bed and crept to the door to look through the security peephole. Seeing no one, I opened the door and stuck my head out. The hallway was empty with the exception of a small calico cat sleeping at the end of the hall under a window. Odd indeed!

It was early Sunday morning, July 15, and I was wide awake and ready to move! *Ugh! Even on vacation I can't sleep in,* I muttered silently to myself. It was only six o'clock in the morning, and I was ready to explore. By six fifteen, while my friend slept, I was up, dressed in my hiking attire, and out on the fourth-floor observation balcony known as Dr. Baker's Lounge Patio. Saint Elizabeth's Church could be seen clearly one level below the hotel at 30 Crescent Drive. Beyond the church and continuing down the mountain, picturesque Victorian houses were nestled secretly amidst the dense forest and mostly invisible due to the thick trees and foliage. I imagined that in only a few months, the leaves would change from their shades of greens to brilliant oranges, yellows, and browns before dropping to provide full view of the historic village.

In particular, I noticed the few clouds above me in the early morning blue sky and one small cloud hovering below where I stood, shielding my view of the village below. The universe and Earth Mother had given me a second front-row seat for their magnificent production. I wanted to take full advantage of this once-in-a-lifetime opportunity and go for a walk between the clouds. The universe was again sending me a message, and I was listening. I was totally unaware that in three short days, I would collapse with a severe brain bleed that would completely change my life forever.

Within a few minutes, I made a quick visit to our room, found Mary Lou still peacefully sleeping, picked up my camera, grabbed a cup of coffee from the lobby, and was outside breathing in the fresh mountain air. I had only walked a few yards when an odd little bird joined me. (Figure 6.5) I took a few snapshots of this marvelous little creature that was running along on the ground, sometimes running ahead and then stopping, as if waiting for me to catch up with him before darting off again. I turned to the left and walked down a steep stone pathway to Crescent Drive and Saint Elizabeth's Church. I noticed a sign at the entrance of a pathway—Magnolia Path. There was an immediate familiarity to the sign, accompanied by a strong desire to cross the street and enter the trail.

Figure 6.5 Rudy the Roadrunner

As I stood considering both the sign and the thickly forested trail beyond, I rationalized that the familiar feeling was due to the sign itself. My family had lived in Mobile, Alabama, (The Azalea City) for nearly eighteen years, and while there, we often participated in the annual Azalea Trail 10K Run. This sign, with its picture of a blooming magnolia, looked very much like the azaleas I had grown to love. I quickly determined that I was only imagining an invitation from the universe to enter this particular trail, and then my thoughts became engulfed in a huge debate. My inner voice was screaming at me to enter this beautiful paradise, while my ego voice was logically pointing out that the trail would only take me back into a town that I had already visited. I had not yet learned to completely listen to my inner voice, so I allowed the ego to prompt me to continue my adventure in a totally opposite direction.

I turned around, climbed back up the stone steps, and was joined once again by my little feathered friend. We traveled together side by side through East Garden, and as I was making the turn toward the front of the hotel, he bid his farewell and returned to where we first met. *I later discovered that my hiking partner was the famous* Rudy the Roadrunner *who had been the subject of a feature article in the local newspaper. His claim to fame is because he is a southwestern species rarely found in this part of Arkansas. I was overjoyed to have been blessed with the companionship of such a wonderful little creature.*

As I entered a pathway leading down and away from the west side of the hotel, I felt very alone without the company of my little bird friend. At that moment, I thought about my iPod, which was lying on the dresser in our room, and realized that I would not be able to listen to my walking music. I immediately began yoga deep breathing exercises and entered into a walking meditation to thank God and the universe for the opportunity of experiencing Earth Mother's nature as it was intended. As I walked, I mentally surrounded myself with the white light of love and divine protection. I prayed that I could experience only positive thoughts and energies and that I would not be affected by any negative energy that I might encounter. I soon realized that without the distraction of the music that I usually listen to, I was able to more deeply enjoy the sounds of nature and became more aware of everything around me. The longer I walked, the more at peace I became.

I am one of those people who seems to have a built-in clock, which is a blessing most times, but it can also be a curse, especially when I would like to sleep late and cannot. This internal clock was now telling me that I had been walking for approximately an hour and should be heading back to the hotel. I was, at the time, walking on an isolated clay service road and had started feeling a little uncomfortable and vulnerable. I reversed my direction and made my way back to the paved mountain roadway where I turned left and began following the downhill incline. In no time, I found myself once again in front of St. Elizabeth's Church with the hotel sitting immediately on the upper crest to my right. As I left the roadway to climb the rock stairway back up to the hotel, I froze where I stood on the second step.

I knew that I should be going back to the hotel, but for a very strong and unexplained reason, I was once again being called to the Magnolia Path behind me. This time, the pull was much stronger than earlier. *What was beckoning me to enter this path? Was this a divine guidance? Was the universe talking to me again?* I stood with my back to it for a few minutes before finally saying aloud, "All right, I'm coming."

As soon as I entered the secluded trail, my senses became keenly aware of my surroundings. This was one of the most beautiful places I had ever experienced. Streams of early morning sunlight were only slightly breaking through the thick growth of trees, and the sweet smell of morning air had enveloped me. Almost immediately a deer appeared a few feet ahead and stopped. We stood in place looking at each other for what seemed to be an eternity. Its almond brown eyes warmly welcomed me and seemed to be saying, "At last I have found you. What took you so long?" I gently raised my camera and snapped a shot. We watched each other for several more long minutes, and then as softly as it had appeared, it turned and walked gently down into the valley. I was left in a heightened state of serenity and continued on the winding pathway.

The narrow walkway wrapped to the right around a deep crevice filled with an overgrowth of plants and small trees before opening into a neighborhood of Victorian homes. As I neared the clearing, I took one last picture looking back at the tranquil trail behind me. I continued down the hill until I arrived at a small park, Grotto Spring, on the outskirts of the town. I took a few additional pictures and, being aware of the time, turned around and followed my footsteps back to the hotel. Mary Lou was awake, showered, dressed, and waiting for my return.

"I was beginning to worry about you."

"You should have been with me!" I exclaimed. "I have never felt as relaxed and at peace as I did this morning."

"I'm glad, and you can tell me all about it later. I want to see the pictures, but right now, get ready to go. I thought we could have lunch in one of the quaint little restaurants in town."

"Sounds good to me." I was already heading for the shower.

"I'll be waiting for you outside on the observation deck."

Chapter Seven

A Spiritual Greeting

"Nature: trees, flowers, and grass grow in silence;
The stars, the moon, and the sun move in silence ...
In silence He listens to us; in silence He speaks to our souls."[9]
Mother Teresa

Within thirty minutes, I had taken a quick shower and met Mary Lou outside on Dr. Baker's Observation Deck. We sat for only a few minutes making our day's plan before catching a trolley to the historic downtown district. Realizing the steep incline of the town's streets, we asked the trolley driver to drop us off at the highest stop in the business district. We would then leisurely take our time exploring the shops as we made our way down into the center of town; after all, it is much easier to walk downhill than the reverse.

Mary Lou's shopping quest for unusual home decorating items resulted in our visiting a myriad of unique boutiques. Following a few hours of walking and shopping, a park bench caught Lou's attention so that she could rest her feet, and I was attracted to a nearby Oriental gift shop. No sooner had I walked through the door when the proprietor, a middle-aged

---

9 Mother Teresa, and Thomas Moore. *No Greater Love* (Novato: New World Library, 2002), 10.

lady of Chinese origin, warmly greeted me as though I were an old friend for whom she had been waiting.

"Welcome! Come in!"

"Hello. Your shop is beautiful."

"You've been here before?" Her question sounded more like a statement. "We have already met. Yes?"

"No, I don't believe we have. But then, haven't we all met sometime before ... in a past life?" I don't usually say this to complete strangers and couldn't believe that I had now.

"Yes," she smiled. "We are all family."

We both giggled as I began looking at her collection of Buddha statues. "I have something which I brought back from China for you." As she was talking, she removed a small package from a drawer and handed me a delicate silver medal. It resembled a Catholic medal of the blessed Mother.

"What does this represent?" I inquired.

"This is Quan Yin. She is a Bodhisattva. In the teachings of Buddha, she is an enlightened one who seeks to help others become enlightened."

I gazed down at the dainty silver medal positioned in the center of my palm.

"She is all compassion and loving kindness, and she will bless you with physical and spiritual peace."

Physical and spiritual peace? Who couldn't use more of that? "How much?" I asked.

"Nothing. This is my gift to you. You will wear it and be safe. Yes?"

I could not believe that this total stranger would be handing me such a beautiful gift. "Yes, I will wear it proudly."

Before leaving the store, I purchased a silver chain for Quan Yin. As I walked to the door, I turned to thank her. She smiled at me and bowed. I bowed in return. My heart warmed, and once again, I knew that the universe had guided me to be in that particular store at that exact moment. I rarely take the necklace off, and since that day, I have had the opportunity to educate many others about the powers of Quan Yin.

I returned to where Mary Lou was waiting to show her my gift and to share the story of Quan Yin.

"This would only happen to you," she said laughingly.

We walked two blocks down Spring Street before finding an enchanting little open-air restaurant. Even in the mountains, Arkansas gets hot in the middle of July, and we were hot, hungry, and very thirsty. We placed our orders for chicken sandwiches and iced tea before sitting at a small table located under a rustic outdoor ceiling fan.

"Okay, let's see the pictures you took this morning," Mary Lou said.

"My pleasure." I was already digging the camera out of my backpack. I had taken many pictures while I was hiking that morning; I also had not had an opportunity to look at them myself. Our iced tea was being delivered to the table as I tapped on the power button.

We were reviewing pictures of the outside of the hotel, Morris the cat's grave, the roadrunner, the east lawn wedding garden, Saint Elizabeth's Church, and …

"What in the world is this?" I asked while staring at a very blurred picture.

"You're the one that took it," chided my friend.

"No, really! I have no idea what this is … see the deer? This was taken only a minute or two after I entered the Magnolia Path. I don't know why it's so blurry. My little Kodak never takes blurred pictures." (Figure 7.1)

"Well, it did this time."

I clicked to the next picture; the one I took looking back on the trail.

"I can't believe this!" I was becoming upset. This had been the most beautiful part of the hike, and the pictures were ruined.

Mary Lou took the camera and studied the picture closer. "What's this?"

"What? Where?" I asked.

"Here," she said, pointing toward the center of the frame. "Isn't that a person?" (Figure 7.2 and front cover)

"It can't be. I was alone except for the deer. There was absolutely no one else on the trail with me." Very clearly the image of a tall, dark-haired, faceless woman wearing a long, black dress had appeared in the center of the picture. Everything else was a blur of pastel colors.

Figure 7.1 Deer on Magnolia Path

I clicked back to the blurred picture of the deer.

"Lou, look! Isn't there someone in this picture also?" I asked, handing her the camera and pointing between two small trees in the foreground.

"Oh my Lord!" she shrieked. "You've got ghost pictures!"

"Could it be?" I was totally overjoyed with the possibility.

She took the camera and forwarded to the "lady" picture. "Pat, look at this again. Isn't there another person in the back center of the picture … just to the right of her head?"

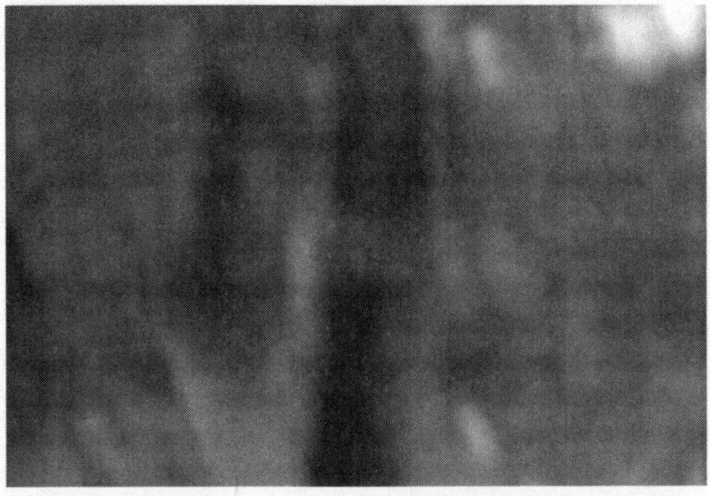

Figure 7.2 Lady on Magnolia Path

"Indeed there is." It appeared more as an X-ray shadow of a man in hues of green, but it was definitely a human form. Over the next few hours, additional figures became visible in both pictures. Whether we had only then noticed them, or they were appearing more with the passing of time is unknown. By the time we returned to the hotel, we had been able to count at least six adult images and one small child sitting in the lower-left corner of the lady picture and three distinct apparitions in the deer photograph."What are you going to do with these?"

"I'm thinking that we'll be waiting outside the ghost tour office when they open and ask them what they think. If they are ghosts, maybe someone there will know who they are. At the least, possibly they've seen pictures similar to these." I was beyond excited, and I could not wait to call Pam.

My mother used to say that a watched pot never boils, and that cliché had never been as true as that evening when we were waiting for the office to open for our seven thirty tour. As soon as we returned to our room, I plugged in the camera to ensure a full charge for the ghost tour. We then drove into town and had an early Italian dinner at Ermilio's, which was only a short drive down the mountain. This would allow us plenty of time to eat and be back at the hotel in time for the tour office to open.

We returned to the hotel at around six fifteen and decided that we still had enough time to freshen up before the tour began. Earlier, Mary Lou had placed bath towels and a few items of folded clothing on the large window ledge in the bathroom. When she picked up the shirt, which she was planning to wear, she discovered that everything was soaking wet. The towels and her clothes had been nowhere near water, and it definitely had not rained; however, everything looked and felt as though it had just been removed from a washing machine that had skipped the spin cycle. Had someone entered our room while we were away and done something to cause this? We never arrived at a reasonable explanation as to how this might have happened.

A dozen or so guests had already gathered outside the office at approximately seven twenty-five when our two guides arrived and opened the door. I waited for three people to purchase their tickets before entering.

"Hello, I'm Patricia Leffingwell, and I'm staying here as a guest."

"Welcome, Patricia. I'm Ken. Do you need to sign up for tonight's tour?"

"Actually, we already have tickets."

"Great! What else can I do for you?"

I handed my camera to him describing briefly where I had taken the pictures. "Can you tell me anything about this picture? Do you have any idea who this might be?"

He looked at it for a few seconds and then handed it to the man seated next to him saying, "Carroll is our expert and much better suited to answer your question."

Immediately upon looking at it, Carroll asked me to tell him exactly where I was when I took the picture.

"I've seen many pictures taken by our guests, but I've never seen anything like what you have here."

My heart was pounding.

He continued, "Do you meditate?"

"Yes."

"Then I would suggest that you meditate and see if you can open communication with this woman. Possibly, she will tell you who she is and let you know why she has made herself visible to you." He then handed the camera back to me continuing with, "Spirits make themselves visible to people for different reasons. It's obvious that she has chosen you. It's altogether possible that she has something important that only you can know. You will have to learn for yourself what that message is."

Immediately, I began hearing Reverend Zanghi's message, *You were scheduled to die, but the universe has changed.* Was there a connection?

Chapter Eight

Full Circle

"You have noticed that everything an Indian does is in a circle, and that is because the Power of the world always works in circles, and everything tries to be round.... The life of a man is a circle from childhood to childhood, and so it is in everything where power moves."[10]

Black Elk

A young couple, their three-year-old son, and the husband's parents arrived late, making it slightly before eight o'clock by the time we began the ghost tour. My head was filling with pressure again as we were standing in the hallway waiting. I wondered if possibly I was simply overly tired, having the onset of a migraine, or actually feeling the energies of nearby spirits. I was hoping it was spirit getting my attention.

The guides, Ken and Carroll, began the tour just outside their office where we were gathered. They shared with us the horrific history when Dr. Norman Baker occupied the hotel. We were told of the hotel closing during the Great Depression and how the townspeople were so happy when he moved his hospital to Eureka Springs. They were hoping this would bring a much needed improvement to their dwindling economy. Dr. Baker raised most of his money through mail-order marketing of his cure for cancer, boasting no surgery and a high recovery rate. Obviously, he did not want

10 Neihardt, 194–95.

word to spread that patients were dying from his experimental formula, so he gave orders to keep the dead in their rooms until the hospital had closed each day. An apparition of a nurse pushing a gurney down the hall and vanishing into thin air is often seen and heard by guests. Many believe she is a nurse transporting deceased patients to the basement incinerator. A few hotel workers have told of sightings of Dr. Baker wandering through the hallways late at night dressed in his trademark purple suit.

There have been many reported sightings of a well-dressed gentleman in 1890s clothing. He is always described as having dark hair, sporting muttonchops sideburns, and wearing a top hat. Most frequently, he has been seen in the hotel lobby and gift shop, but on occasion, he has appeared in the Crystal Dining Room Restaurant. While the hotel has a vast collection of historic pictures, the identity of this distinguished gentleman has never been confirmed.

The second floor, we were told, seems to have more reported incidences of ghosts than anywhere else in the hotel. Several hotel employees and guests have seen Michael, the Irish stone worker who fell to his death in 1885 during construction of the hotel. Michael died in the area that is now known as room 218, one of the most spiritually active rooms in the hotel. One employee, while working in the laundry, said that Michael appeared so often that he became a nuisance and interfered with her work.

Ken told us of how two couples, determined to discredit the Michael stories, checked in and requested room 218. Planning to hold a séance, the two women and two men locked themselves in with a Ouija board and plenty of alcoholic beverages and ordered room service—vowing not to leave the room under any circumstances. As the evening passed, the girls became frightened of sounds they began hearing and felt they were being touched by something unseen. They finally left, begging their dates to leave with them. The men, who remained in 218 drinking heavily, began calling for Michael's spirit to show himself. At around two o'clock in the morning, the Ouija planchette began rapidly moving itself around the board. The startled men watched as the planchette flew off the board and circled the room before finally making its way through an open window. At this point, the hysterical men ran out of the room, down the stairway, through the lobby, and out into the parking lot, vowing never to return. The hotel staff later packed their belongings and held them in the lobby. The suitcases were ultimately retrieved by someone other than one of the foursome.

While the second floor seems to have more frequent reports of spiritual activity, there are reported sightings throughout the hotel and on the surrounding grounds. We learned that the fourth floor wing, the location of our room, was used as a nursery for the children cancer patients. This validated what our bellman told us the day before. Ken continued by saying that many guests report hearing children running in the hall, and others tell stories of their doors being played with during the night. This was definitely an ah-ha moment for me, because I had been awakened at three in the morning by the rattling doorknob.

I poked Mary Lou in her ribs with my finger. "See, I told you something was happening this morning!"

"Next time, I want you to wake me. I miss all the good stuff."

"Mary Lou, I have never been able to wake you up. Even in high school when Becky and I were standing outside your window beating on the glass, you would not wake up. You snooze … you lose!"

"Ha-ha, very funny. At least try. Okay?"

Mary Lou and I also wondered about her wet clothing, which we had only recently discovered. Could this have also been a child's prank?

Our group descended the carpeted stairway leading to the basement, the former location of Dr. Baker's morgue. Mary Lou was obviously nervous about going there, but she was a trooper and hung in there with me. Once we reached the basement level, we turned and walked through an extremely narrow hall that ran the entire width of the hotel. The hall emptied into the morgue, which, much to my surprise, was not very large and was composed of several small rooms. With the exception of the entry room, lighting was only from bare bulbs hanging from the ceiling by electric wires. There was a damp, old, musty smell that is common in structures of this age.

We were shown the former location of the incinerators used to burn the bodies of those unfortunate souls not claimed by their families. We then moved on to the refrigeration room. During the Dr. Baker era, this was where bodies and body parts of deceased patients were stored until being used in the doctor's many and sordid experiments. I walked into the cramped space of the body parts room with two other guests. Mary Lou preferred to remain with the rest of our group. The three of us agreed that there was an unsettling and deeply sad feeling associated with being there. There was no doubt that it was felt by each one of us the moment we stepped inside. We remained in the room for only a few minutes before rejoining the rest of the tour.

Even before Ken began telling of the morgue's strong energies, I became aware of the pressure pounding in my head once again. The air flow was not the best, so I deduced that what I was feeling was a lack of air combined with the body heat generated by so many people in our group. I remember asking Mary Lou if she felt any pressure or had any problems breathing. She did not, but she did admit that the room was rather warm and that she was starting to feel tired. I then noticed that the lighting began to appear almost aura-like in that everyone seemed to have become encased in a white shadowy glow. I rationalized that it was my weary eyesight combined with the light of the bare bulbs. However, what happened next made me question that rationalization.

We gathered closely together in the one well-lit room, and Ken cautioned us about our cameras and other electronic equipment. In the past, many people had complained of their camera batteries being drained while in this particular location. *It is believed that since spirits are pure energy, they strengthen themselves by drawing energy from other sources. Camera batteries are one of the easiest sources for them to access.* I looked at my freshly charged camera with its full battery icon and was pleased with myself for charging it while we were at dinner.

Ken began telling of the many spirits that had been photographed around the hotel and then announced that someone in our group had had an interesting photographic experience earlier that morning. He looked directly at me and asked if I would mind sharing my story. I was happy to relate one of the most unusual experiences of my life—especially to an interested and like-minded audience, even if we were standing in the middle of this 1930s morgue. As to be expected, everyone wanted to see the pictures. I had just brought up the picture of the lady when my camera automatically turned itself off, along with the cameras belonging to two people standing next to me. I was able to power it on again only for another brief moment. It remained powered on long enough for another guest to take a picture of my picture before both of our cameras turned themselves off. Ken reminded us that this was not at all uncommon in the morgue.

Was there a connection between the odd glowing appearance of the lighting, which I had noticed only minutes before, and the loss of battery charges we were now experiencing? I found it odd that no one else mentioned the appearance of the lighting. Had I been the only one who noticed it?

Our experienced guides always scheduled the tour to end in the morgue, primarily due to the loss of camera charges, which was understandable. We walked together back through the darkened, narrow hallway and stood at the bottom of the stairway leading up to the main lobby. We were told that the official tour had ended, but we were encouraged to continue exploring on our own if we chose to do so. Mary Lou was looking suspiciously at me, knowing all to well that I would want to continue.

We stopped briefly in our room so that I could recharge my camera. Oddly, as I was about to place it in its charger, I noticed that the battery icon was full! My little Kodak was working fine. So, what had caused all of our cameras to fail—and fail at the exact same time?

Mary Lou and I went back outside to Dr. Baker's Observation Deck and relaxed, taking in the clear, sweet, nighttime, mountain air. We exchanged a few ghost stories from previous excursions with a man and his son who had also been on our tour before saying goodnight and retiring to our room. It was then that I found myself wishing that we were staying longer. I was very comfortable in this surrounding and definitely was not ready to leave.

As Mary Lou began organizing her suitcase and getting ready for bed, I announced, "Since my camera is working again, I'm going back downstairs to take a few more pictures."

"I'm not surprised, but be careful!" she said in a motherly tone.

"I'm not going to be long. I promise."

"You're not going back down to the morgue are you?"

Without a pause, I quickly responded, "No." We both laughed.

"Good! I would worry about you if you went down there by yourself."

"Yes, Mother!" I joked. "We need to get an early start tomorrow, so I promise I won't be long. I'd like to get up early enough in the morning to walk the Magnolia Path one last time. Maybe I can see my tree people again."

Mary Lou looked at me cautiously, "Are you sure that's a good idea?"

"What could possibly happen? Who knows? Maybe I can even talk to her this time? Do you want to come?"

Mary Lou rolled over, pulled the covers over her head, and groaned, "Take your key with you!"

"I guess that's a no. See you in the morning!" I said laughingly.

As soon as I locked the door behind me, I walked the stairwell straight back downstairs to the basement level. I stood looking at the hallway leading to the morgue and took a picture into the darkness, which seemed more like a black hole. "No way am I coming back into the morgue. Not again. Once tonight was enough for me! You will have to enjoy it without me." I said out loud to any spirit energy that might be listening.

I reversed the direction I was facing and went into the ladies' locker room. After about five minutes of taking random pictures, I suddenly felt as though I was not alone after all. I had another shuddering chill that caused me to shiver. I quickly made my way back into the hallway, and as soon as the door closed behind me, I turned and took two pictures in succession. The first picture (Figure 8.1) seemed to be a large orb in motion and was moving away from the door I had just exited. The second (Figure 8.2), taken a split second after the first, showed only the wall. No orbs anywhere. I stood there for several minutes looking at the pictures, then at the wall, and then back to the pictures again. I knew I was not alone in that locker room. Whatever spirit was there had followed me through the door and into the hallway.

Figure 8.1 Orb in Motion

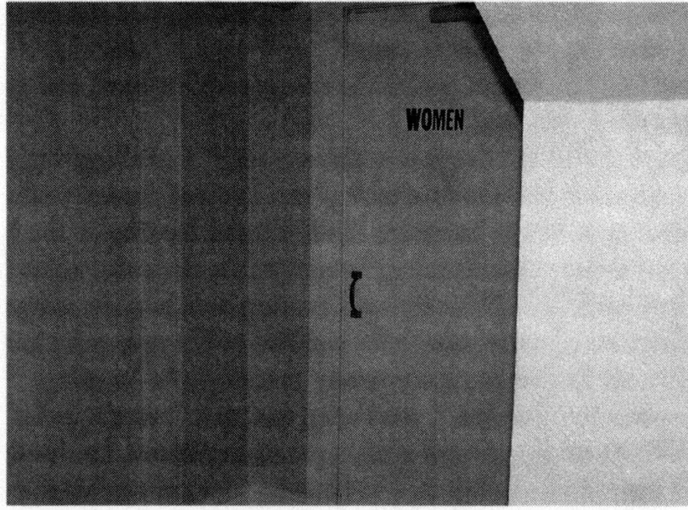

Figure 8.2 Orb Vanished

I sat down on a step at the foot of the stairwell studying the pictures and trying to absorb what had just happened. As I studied the pictures, I began to wonder if there was only one orb spirit, or if there were several energies traveling together and watching me.

Earlier that evening, while still at the ghost tour office, Carroll Heath suggested that I take multiple shots if I suspected that spirit was present. He said that if both pictures show the same thing, then there is probably a physical cause for the picture. It is when something appears in one shot and not in the second that a phenomenon has occurred. These pictures were definitely not the same.

As usual, my built-in alarm woke me right on schedule. I silently rolled out of bed and dressed trying not to wake Mary Lou. I found this funny since she sleeps so soundly, but nevertheless, I was being a good friend and did not want to wake her too early. Unlike the previous day, I did not take a leisurely stroll around the hotel, and I wasn't greeted by my new feathered friend, Rudy the Roadrunner. Being aware of the fact that we would be checking out in only a few hours, I quickly did a brief meditation as I headed straight for the Magnolia Path. I walked all the way into town taking pictures at almost every turn, but unfortunately, I was unable to capture photos of the deer, the lady, or any of the other spirits from the day before. I returned to the hotel feeling like I had missed saying good-bye to close friends.

As we were checking out, I decided to show my pictures to the staff working at the front desk. They pulled out a photo album filled with spirit pictures taken by both staff and other guests. Nothing resembling my mysterious lady was to be found. They asked if I would send them copies of my pictures for the hotel's collection once I returned home.

We said good-bye to this Grand Old Lady of the Ozarks and drove back to Mary Lou's home in North Little Rock. As should be expected, we chatted all the way about our experiences and the fact that I had taken such remarkable pictures. Mary Lou opened up to me that she often feels her deceased mother's presence. She asked me to take pictures that night around her house to see if any spirit might be there. I'm sorry to say that nothing appeared on my camera that night.

Early the next morning, July 17, we got up early and grabbed a fast food breakfast en route to Little Rock National Airport. We made a quick stop so that I could purchase a book about the history of North Little Rock before visiting Little Rock's National Cemetery where both my mother and father are buried. We entered the beautiful rolling hills of the cemetery with its well manicured grounds lined with rows and rows of sparkling white head markers. We drove to the section where my parents' marker is located and parked. As I opened the car door, I was overcome with a feeling of great sadness. The feeling was so intense that before I could even walk to their marker, I was overcome and began shaking and became hysterical with tears.

What is this? I asked myself. I miss my parents tremendously, but I knew that this emotion was not about them. Whatever had taken over me was much more powerful than anything I had ever felt. It was a combination of sadness and intense anger. Arriving at their headstone seemed to have a calming effect, and then as I turned to walk back to the car, the shaking and tears began again. Mary Lou helped me getting back into the car.

"Are you okay, Honey?"

"I think so. I don't know what that was."

"It's very hard to go to the cemetery for a parent," she said, consoling me.

"No, it's not that. It's like something grabbed me as soon as I opened the door. It wasn't seeing my parents' marker that did this."

"This is really weird."

"I know. Did you read any of those markers near the car? Some of them were from the 1800s and early 1900s. There are so many lost souls here. I'm afraid that as sensitive as I've become, something attached itself to me. It was so sad! It was like it wasn't me that was crying but someone else using my body to cry!"

"Okay, now you are really starting to freak me out. Are you okay to go to the airport? Your flight will be boarding soon."

As she started the car and drove out of the cemetery, I became myself again. The shaking and crying stopped instantly. The deep sadness and anger that had overtaken me were immediately gone. I soon realized that in my haste to pack and leave, I had neither prayed nor meditated that morning. I had walked into that cemetery completely unprotected by the white light of love and divine protection, thereby leaving myself completely vulnerable to any spirit energy—good or bad.

Mary Lou was correct; my plane was preparing to board as I approached the gate, but then the attendant announced that due to storms between Little Rock and Memphis, our flight would be delayed. I relaxed in the airport terminal by sipping a cappuccino and called my husband, who was waiting for me in New Orleans. He said that our daughter Kimberly and her family were on their way from Mobile and that they should be there by the time I arrived. I had not seen Ralph in more than a week and was also looking forward to being with Kimberly and her family. Together we would all enjoy three wonderful days in New Orleans.

Life was good, and I was feeling on top of the world. In less than twenty-four hours, I would collapse with a life-threatening hematoma followed by three brain surgeries. However, on that particular day, while waiting patiently in the airport terminal, my memories of recent experiences combined with my expectations of what was yet to be discovered in New Orleans. Nothing could have been further from my thoughts than the words spoken by Reverend Don Zanghi seven months earlier...."You were scheduled to die, but the universe has changed."

Part Two

"Study as if you have not reached your goal—hold it as if you were afraid of losing what you have."

Confucius

Keeping Your Psychic Journal

You may have already experienced flashbacks of psychic or spiritual encounters as you were reading Part One. *Congratulations if you did! I was hoping that you would.* Allowing yourself to become more consciously aware and accepting of these events is necessary if you want to develop your own psychic senses. A key step toward a higher awareness is by keeping a journal. If my 2007 journey triggered one or more memories for you, begin right now by writing them down. Include as many details as you can remember.

As you progress through the remaining chapters, continue to jot down other memories as they arise. It does not matter how small the events may seem at the time. At the conclusion of each chapter, you will be given an opportunity to think, reflect, and journal your thoughts and recollections.

Write freely in your journal, and do not worry about style, grammar, or spelling. The important thing is to write. The more you journal, the easier it becomes. Your inner self—your mind and soul—will, by all appearances, begin to dictate messages to you. Write down these thoughts or messages as you receive them. Be prepared that some messages may not make sense at the time you receive them. Write them down anyway. Everything happens for a reason, and even the oddest message may make perfect sense in the future.

Happy journaling!

Chapter Nine

Soul Searching

Understanding mysteries must come little by little, otherwise you may become lost forever in the unknown.

Years have come and gone since Reverend Zanghi delivered Dr. Huxley's message. At the time, the message seemed odd and even a little spooky, but it did not propel me into a depressed or schizophrenic panic. I honestly interpreted the message as describing something that was to have happened in the past. It was only after my surgeries that I began taking a closer look at life and my purpose for living it and began constructing a list of questions.

- When we die, where do our souls, memories, and personalities go?
- Does our true essence simply cease to exist as professed by many traditional scientists?
- What exactly is this thing called the spiritual universe?
- Is the spiritual universe another plane of existence?
- Is it a separate universe where our innermost energies continue to live following the death of our physical forms?
- If our spirits continue to exist, how then is it possible for some people to communicate with souls in this other dimension but not everyone?

My undergraduate years were at a research intensive university, and thanks to that educational background, research is something that I both know and enjoy. How difficult would it be, I wondered, for me to unearth facts about what the universe actually is? I became determined that I would find answers to all of my current questions and any others as they materialized; my infinite quest for knowledge launched on the third day following my hospital release. As I look back on it now, what I had actually done was to accept the challenge of discovering the true meaning of the universe. Hmmm? Had that not been tried before?

Thank goodness for the invention of laptop computers! While I may have been restricted to the sofa for several weeks, it did not stop me from surfing the Internet as I searched for books and other publications pertaining to my research topics. Almost daily the postman or other carrier would deliver another book or two to my front doorstep. Before I realized it, I had developed quite an impressive library in my little home office.

I quickly confirmed that I was not the first person to ask what the universe is. The topic has been around since the beginning of time, and many of our greatest scientific and philosophical minds had already asked the same questions. I first confirmed that conceptually there are *at least* two universes: the physical universe and a spiritual universe. Second, these two completely separate entities operate independently but can communicate and interact under the right conditions. I also gained valuable insights as to how these two universes working together may have affected my own experiences.

I began my research by seeking a definition of the noun *universe* and found numerous variations. Merriam-Webster.com listed the history, or etymology, as a Middle English word dating back to the fourteenth century. Definitions include "the whole body of things and phenomena observed or postulated: a systematic whole held to arise by and persist through the direct intervention of divine power; the world of human experience; and the entire celestial cosmos."

Allwords.com defines the universe as a proper noun that means "The sum of everything that exists in the cosmos, including time and space." While another definition offered by EnchantedLearning.com, which I found to be much more simplistic and yet all encompassing, is "The universe is everything, all matter and energy that is in existence." Having identified a few acceptable definitions, I wanted to know how this vast space holding all things and phenomena, both matter and energy, could directly communicate with us living on this planet.

My search for explanations began by examining theories surrounding the creation of Earth and all other planets and elements that we refer to as the physical universe. It did not take long before I realized that the majority of what I was reading was based on established, set in stone, scientific principles and laws. For something to be proven scientifically, a scientist will first form a theory as to how or why something behaves in a certain way and then develop a hypothesis, a statement of what is believed will be the outcome of the experiments. Through a series of controlled tests and observations, the results will then prove the hypothesis as being either true or false. This may work well for the tangible elements of the physical universe, but what about the spiritual universe—that invisible space containing the intangible elements of thoughts, beliefs, dreams, faith, and our souls? Physical science alone was not able to produce answers to these questions.

Much to my mother's chagrin, I was born feet first into this world. Now here I was naively jumping feet first into another world—the world of quantum physics. It was never my plan to enter this scientific arena, but as I was taught decades ago: you do not lead the research; the research leads you. It would be impossible to complete this topic without examining the thoughts of the world's leading quantum physicists. It is not important that we decide who is right and who is wrong in their arguments; however, it is interesting to trace the history and scholarly thoughts about the universe(s). I confess to you that this was a most difficult chapter for me to write. Not only was I researching in an area totally outside my field of study and comfort zone, but the fact is that the arguments and debates over the creation of the universe, spiritual or otherwise, are still unresolved. However, I did find the history of scholarly arguments quite interesting and, at times, even amusing.

Much of our modern scientific thinking has its metaphysical and philosophical roots tracing back to the ancient Greeks. It was these early scientists who first conceived the theories of the prima materia, or the basic element(s) from which our universe was created. Early scientific thinkers, such as Thales, Heraclitus, Anaximander, Pythagoras Parmenides, Empedocles, and Aristotle, introduced their theories between the years of 610–384 BC. It was with Empedocles's writing *On Nature* (mid-fifth century BC) that the four elements of antiquity—earth, air, fire, and water—were first introduced. The belief that everything was formed from these four elements remained for two thousand years until modern science developed new insights. It is interesting to note that those original four elements written about by Empedocles still serve as symbols for our modern states of matter—solids, liquids, gases, and plasma.

Being a nonscientist, I found it most interesting to discover Democritus's theory, which stated that if we continually divide a piece of matter until we reach a point that it can no longer be divided, we end up with an atom. Democritus made this discovery somewhere around 440 BC! Not only was I not the first person to question the origin of the universe (*surprise!*), but these ancient scientists had actually uncovered complex elements such as atoms. How was this possible without the invention of microscopes and other modern scientific equipment? Had the universe spoken to them and guided their findings? Very interesting indeed!

In his book *The Spiritual Universe*, Fred Alan Wolf, PhD, described an ancient scientific belief, very similar to our big bang theory of today, which speculated that the universe was formed from a vast void or vacuum. The ancients believed that the Creator could not be found in only one specific location but was, in fact, a part of everything in nature and the universe, which is continually forming.[11]

Dr. Wolf admitted in his chapter "Some Soulful but Wrong Questions" that it was difficult for him, as a scientist, to seek any scientific proof of the soul. He confessed that his knowledge is a gift when it comes to scientifically examining the physical world, but this same knowledge is a curse when trying to study and explain a nontangible thing such as the soul. He continued by saying that he is envious of the unscientific minds that blindly accept spiritual truths.[12] Modern science has only recently begun to question those elements that are unseen and unobservable.

The more I read about the different theories, the more I began to realize that there are definitely at least two completely different realms. First there is our outer, physical universe in which we live and work, and second, there is our inner universe where we think and dream—the heartbeat of our souls. How then do these two somewhat opposite universes interact or communicate with each other?

Ironically, it was following a meditation one afternoon that I had an ah-ha moment and began to more clearly understand. It was not a message I received during the meditation that provided the clarity; it was the actual act of meditating. *Does this sound a tiny bit odd? If it does, please keep reading. Don't give up on me now.* A basic principle of quantum

---

11 Fred Allen Wolf, PhD, The Spiritual Universe, (Needham: Moment Point Press, 1999), 62.

12 Ibid., 6.

physics states that an electron known as X can leave point A and without any physical movement is able to disappear then reappear at point B in the form of Y. *Keep reading—please do not put the book down. I promise this will make sense.*

Allow me to explain by using my meditation as an example. I was sitting alone in my living room, and through the process of my mind's eye, I saw and felt myself drifting in the warm, blue water of the Pacific. I knew instantly that I was snorkeling off the shore of Maui. Behind my closed eyes, I saw and felt the soothing water caressing my skin as I floated along effortlessly behind a giant sea turtle. Schools of fish were lazily passing by, seemingly unaware of my presence. The water was deep but also so clear that rays of the sun bounced along the sandy bottom, highlighting the green vegetation that danced in the smooth current. Suddenly, out of nowhere I heard a deep roaring sound. At first I thought it was a power boat passing by overhead, but then I quickly realized that I was indeed alone. The sound I was hearing was the voice of a giant humpback whale singing a song of love to its mate. I knew that I had been blessed by hearing this love ballad with my own ears, and I was so touched by the sound that all previous stresses and worries I'd had were instantaneously gone. I was one with nature and at total peace. Then, as gently as I had drifted into this tranquil, underwater sanctuary, I opened my eyes and returned to my original surroundings.

While physically I never left my living room, I had experienced traveling nearly five thousand miles away and had snorkeled in the Pacific Ocean with the humpback whales. My physical body now felt as if I actually had walked out of the sea and had been lying in total relaxation on the beach for hours. In addition, my stress and the tension of the day had completely disappeared; I was a new, improved version of myself for having made the trip. This is quantum physics at work.

In the beginning, I was sitting in my outer universe (living room: point A), and then mentally, I traveled to my inner universe (Maui) before returning to my outer universe (living room: point B) again. One might argue that this whole trip was in my mind only, but quantum physicists call this inner universe our inner space. This is the same principle that explains how in dreams you may visit another location, solve a work-related problem or even relive a special moment in your life, and never leave the comfort of your own personal space.

I cannot tell you how many hours I spent reading and rereading this theory before I finally caught on and enjoyed a big ah-ha moment! I had received an education about why and how meditation works to reduce stress. It was now clear to me that by training ourselves to take these mini mental vacations through meditation, we are able to restore our healthy physical and emotional states of being rested, relaxed, and calm—free of stress. Remember that most, if not all, of what we consider stressful is actually only stressful due to our perceptions and beliefs.

One of the subjects that scientists all now agree upon is the fact that we each have our own individual energy fields. Sometimes this energy is referred to as Chi or an aura. In the not so distant past, medical doctors denied the existence of these bodily energy centers. Today, more and more practitioners are recommending forms of energy healing through Reiki or other therapies that target these energy centers, or chakras. By keeping our chakras balanced, we are able to sustain good health. Likewise, if these centers are out of balance, we might begin to feel depressed or fatigued, become ill, or experience any number of unhealthy symptoms or maladies.

Studies of brainwave activities have identified distinct energy changes when we are sleeping and dreaming. These same changes can be noted while we are fully awake daydreaming or meditating. In his book, *The Vibrational Universe*, Kenneth James Michael MacLean describes our consciousness as being similar to that of a computer operating system in how it transmits or receives bits of energy, or quanta, from the universe. Not only do we allow positive or negative energies to affect us personally, but we also have the power to change our lives by how we process these energies.

I have heard psychics and mediums refer to what are called psychic vampires. These people seem to have the uncanny ability of draining your energies simply by walking into the same room. Before their arrival, you may have been in a completely happy mood. These vampires swoop in, dump their negative thoughts, feelings, and energies on unsuspecting you, and then they leave feeling refreshed and happy. You, on the other hand, are left behind feeling depressed beyond belief. Does this sound familiar? I think we have all met people who feed off of our positive energies; sometimes, they are not even people we know. You may simply pass them on the street or be seated next to them in a restaurant and not even be aware that you have been psychically attacked. We will discuss ways of protecting yourself from unwanted energies in "Chapter Fourteen: Ghosts."

French physicist and philosopher Jean E. Charon wrote in *The Unity of Mind & Matter*, "… the universe is not situated exclusively in rational time and space, but is also thinkable by way of an intuitive approach."[13] Back in the day of the ancient Greeks, the spiritual universe was considered strictly a mental function. Many physicists today believe that if we do not open our conscious minds to the spiritual universe, we may never gain admission into that other realm.

No discussion of the universe can be complete without the findings of Albert Einstein, now referred to as the Father of Modern Physics. His 1905 *Special Theory of Relativity* proved that all things in space are made of time and energy, which interfere with one another. In 1915, he added in his *General Theory of Relativity* that, while all things in the universe are created of time and energy, space itself is curved. Scientists later amended that by adding that if space is too curved, one may theoretically cross over to the other side.

Einstein, although a strict scientist in adhering to the scientific laws of making judgments about only what could be seen and observed, was also a philosopher, having religious upbringing and values. I found it profound that these values were addressed in his book *Albert Einstein In His Own Words*. When discussing joint topics of science and religion, he inquired, "Are we not all children of one father, as it is said in religious language? … It is only to the individual that a soul is given."[14]

Of all my research materials, the book that I found to be the most insightful and thought-provoking was *The Seat of the Soul* written by Gary Zukav. Zukav eloquently explains how modern science has historically been operating by using only the five senses, which, by the way, science told us that we have. He describes how we are undergoing an evolutionary change whereby all mankind is moving toward the use of multisenses. It is in this new multisensory era that we are able to see and understand more clearly the unseen elements in the universe(s). I enjoyed many personal ah-ha moments during this reading and ended it with an even greater feeling of appreciation for our inner space. I highly recommend this book to anyone who is seeking a deeper and more meaningful understanding of our human spirit.

---

13 Jean E. Charon, *The Unity of Mind & Matter Part III: The Universe: My Universe*, ARIADNE'S WEB, Volume 2, Number 1 (Dallas: Rayeson Enterprises, Autumn, 1996), 24.

14 Albert Einstein, *Albert Einstein In His Own Words, Out of My Later Years*, (New York: Portland House / Random House Value Publishing, 2000), 209.

Overview

- There exists both a physical universe and a spiritual universe.
- Scientists have only recently begun to acknowledge the spiritual universe.
- The physical universe contains all elements and matter that can be seen and measured.
- The spiritual universe contains the spiritual realms of souls, spirits, angels, ghosts, and other paranormal entities.
- We are a combination of both physical matter and spiritual energy.
- Our energy field is commonly referred to as an aura or Chi.
- We are affected by positive or negative energies, and we have the power to change our lives by how we process these energies.
- Because energy cannot be destroyed, it stands to reason that our personal energy, our souls, live on after our physical bodies die.

Your Psychic Journal:

This chapter discussed both the physical and spiritual universes. You learned that your personal energies can be affected positively and negatively by outside energies that you come into contact with on a daily basis. If a journal topic has not already popped into your mind, ask yourself the following questions.

- Do you remember being around someone who seemed to build up your own positive energy level just by being in the same room?
- Have you ever known someone who you were uncomfortable being around, but you could not determine exactly why you had this feeling? For some reason, the person just seemed to drain your positive energy levels.
- Have your ever felt the energy of a deceased loved one?

- The energy vibrations of certain places can also affect your moods and physical well-being. Can you remember a situation where this may have happened to you?
- Have you ever had a startling revelation or solved a major problem during a dream or meditation?

Think, reflect, and happy journaling!

Chapter Ten

Déjà Vu, Dreams, and Intuition

"Men go abroad to admire the heights of mountains;
the mighty billows of the sea, the broad tides of rivers,
the width of the ocean, and the paths of the stars,
and they pass themselves by."[15]

St. Augustine

"I had the most realistic dream last night," I said to my husband over a Saturday morning coffee.

"Oh? What was that?"

"I dreamed that I was inside an old house, in another time, and I was looking for you."

"Really? I had a dream that I was looking for you, and I was in a house that I have never seen before."

I looked at him as if I had caught him about to play a joke on me. "Oh, really? Well, what did your house look like?" I inquired.

"It was sometime in the past, maybe either the late 1800s or early 1900s. Two-story …"

I cut him off by saying, "Don't tell me anything else." I went immediately to get paper and pencils. Returning, I said, "Okay, you stay on this side

---

15 Saint Augustine, Bishop of Hippo, [translated by Rex Warner], *Confessions of Saint Augustine*, (New Kensington: Whitaker House, 1996), 247.

of the living room and draw the house exactly as you remember it from your dream. I'll sit at the dining room table and do the same. Then we'll compare pictures." He had at one time been a draftsman, so I already knew that his picture would look much better than anything that I could draw. I specialize in stick people drawings.

After only a few minutes, we had both completed our sketches and laid them side by side on the living room coffee table. Ralph, as expected, had included many more details in his drawing, but there was no doubt that we had drawn the exact same house. It was a white, two-story, wooden, simple-looking house with porches wrapping completely around both the upper and lower levels. It appeared to be located in the middle of a flat field and had what looked like one large oak tree on the right side of the house. The tree separated the house from a large barn with a primitive, wooden, flatbed wagon—the type that would have been pulled by a horse—sitting outside.

As we shared the details of our dreams, I vividly recalled being downstairs walking among many people. The women wore simple, floor-length dresses with long sleeves and high necks, but they were not formal in the sense that we think of formal today. This was definitely some type of celebration, maybe a wedding or a birthday. There was no doubt that whatever the occasion, it was it was a joyous affair. The rooms were well-lit, but I cannot remember if the light was from candles or oil lamps, and I am certain there was no electricity in the house. I remember being very frustrated that I could not find Ralph, and I kept moving from person to person asking where he was. He related to me almost the exact same story. The only variation was that while I remember being downstairs looking for him, he told of being upstairs in the house, walking from room to room searching for me.

How is it possible for two people to dream the exact same dream on the same night? Neither of us had ever been in a house like that before we met, and we know that we have never gone anywhere similar to this together. Off and on, throughout the day, we explored possible reasons why this might have happened but were unable to come up with any reasonable explanation. This was twelve years ago, and to this day, everywhere we go, I find myself looking for this house. I do believe that one day I will find it.

Everyone, at some time in his life, has experienced a déjà vu feeling of either having been somewhere before or having met or seen a complete stranger somewhere in the past but knowing that he has not. These déjà vu experiences are usually accompanied by either a warm, comforting feeling or by an unsettling, negative reaction to the person or place. Before learning to listen to my inner voice, I used to try to overcome negative feelings by disregarding what I felt. Each and every time, the outcome of whatever situation I was in had a dreadful outcome. The following story is one that I had not planned to share, but it is important in showing how déjà vu, intuition, and dreams can work together. It also shows how not listening to my inner voice might have placed me in a very dangerous position.

My husband and I once belonged to a golf and swim club. Over a period of years, the club had been bought and sold several times. I clearly remember being introduced to a new owner during one of the management transitions. When we were initially introduced and shook hands, my blood ran cold. I instantly disliked this man, who I will refer to as Jack, and I had no reason for feeling this way. It was a déjà vu encounter, and I intuitively knew that this was an evil man. I had neither met him before that time nor had I ever heard anything about him prior to our meeting. I talked to my husband about my concerns, and he reassured me that he was simply a "good ol' boy" who was just trying to make a living for his family. Over the next couple of years, we had occasions to socially interact with Jack and his wife. I was extremely comfortable with her but could never be at ease around Jack. I always found myself coming up with ways not to be alone with him, even if it was for only a few minutes.

A dream, or nightmare as it should be called, caused me to wake up trembling early one summer morning. The dream began with a telephone call I received from a girlfriend who lived near the club.

"Hello?"

"Pat! Oh my God! Did you hear what happened at the club last night?" She sounded near hysteria.

"Sally? Are you okay? What's wrong?" I was genuinely concerned about my friend. "You sound awful!"

"You haven't heard? Oh, Pat … it's horrible!" She was now openly sobbing into the phone.

"What is it?" I was actually worrying that something had happened to her husband.

"There was a murder at the club last night!" Sally screamed into the phone.

"What? A murder? Who? What happened?"

"Oh, Pat, it's horrible!"

"Sally, calm down and tell me what happened." I tried to ease her enough to tell me what had happened.

"Joe, the night watchman, was killed last night."

"What? Killed? How? Where?" I could not believe what I was hearing.

"They found him in the golf cart shed behind the club. He's dead! There's blood everywhere! Oh my God!"

I was trying to absorb what I was hearing as Sally continued, "Oh, Pat, this is so terrible! The police are still here. They are all over the place. Joe was beaten to death." I could hear the trembling in her voice. "Sam found him!" Sam, her husband, assisted with the management of the golf course. "I've got to go now. The police are here again."

"At your house?" I questioned.

"Yes, they're at the front door. I've got to go. I'll call you later." She hung up.

I knew instantly who was responsible for this outrageous act. It was Jack. How or why, I didn't know, but I knew. I was seeing his smirking, grinning face looking at me and saying, "So what are you going to do about it?" I was terrified and shaking as I awoke and tried as best I could to have a normal morning.

I kissed Ralph good-bye and watched him turn out of the driveway en route to his office. He had only been gone a few minutes when, as I walked into the kitchen, our telephone began to ring.

"Hello?"

"Pat! Oh my God! Did you hear what happened at the club last night?" I squeezed the receiver against my ear listening to my distraught friend, knowing exactly what was to come. Our conversation unfolded, word for word, as it had happened during my dream only a few hours earlier.

From that time forward, I refused to be anywhere that I thought Jack would be. I prayed that the authorities would capture him, bringing this nightmare to an end. I even had thoughts about going to the police, but then I questioned what I would tell them. "I had a dream about the murder and know who the killer is." They surely would lock me up for being mentally unbalanced. This was also before psychics began to be publicly accepted by police departments as a resource in solving crimes; it was also before I became a student of spirituality and learned that we can and do receive humanitarian messages from the universe. At the time this happened, I was terrified. I feared that if I was somehow so connected to this man that I knew he was a killer, then it might also be possible for him to know that I could provide testimony of his involvement with this bloody homicide. All I wanted to do was distance myself to protect my entire family.

The murder became a cold case. Not one suspect was ever arrested for Joe's cold-blooded murder. Almost two years later, Ralph contracted with two men to trim the massive oak trees in our front yard. I carried water to them, and we began talking. Somehow the topic of our club filtered into the conversation. One of them asked, "Wasn't somebody killed there not too long ago?"

I took a deep breath. "Yes, there was."

"Did you know the man that died?" asked one of the workers.

"I knew who he was, but we weren't close enough to be called friends."

They appeared to be very interested in continuing a discussion about that night.

"Do you have any ideas about why he was killed?"

I must have started to appear nervous with the line of questioning by these two complete strangers. For all I knew, they were somehow involved in the murder. Then one of them said, "If you know anything, you should go to the police."

I took a deep breath, "Look, I know this may sound weird, but I had a dream about the murder just before it happened."

"You dreamed it?" they inquired. I was waiting for them to break out laughing, but they did not.

"Yes. So, you see, I don't really know anything. All I did was have a dream."

"Did you see the killer … in your dream?" These guys were persistent in their questioning.

"I'm sorry, but I'm uncomfortable discussing this with you. I've never told anyone about that dream. Why are you so interested, and what makes you think the police would believe me?"

They looked at each other and smiled as they began to understand my nervousness. "Because we're cops." As they said this, they both produced badges from their back pockets. It turned out that they were off-duty policemen who moonlight with their tree trimming business. "We're used to people coming to us with hunches, dreams, feelings, etc. This case hasn't been solved, and any lead would be helpful no matter where it comes from."

I thanked them for being interested and promised that I would consider what they were asking me to do. I never went. Obviously, I have never been able to let the dream go even after so many years have now passed. With my new understanding of psychic phenomena, I often think that maybe I should speak to someone in the police department about the dream, but until that day comes, I will continue to remain quiet about what I know. Writing about it here is a giant step forward.

The purpose of sharing these two dreams is to show that dreams can be a form of psychic vision. The story of the mysterious house can be described as having been a déjà vu experience based on a reincarnation memory from having lived there in a past life. I have been told by three different past life mediums that this is not the first time Ralph and I have been together. In fact, the night we were first introduced, I remember thinking that he was familiar and wondered if we had ever met before. The house dream occurred years before I became a student of spiritualism and developed an understanding of past lives and past life regression. When I was first told that we had been married before, I immediately remembered the house, and the dream suddenly made sense.

The cold case murder dream was another form of psychic vision known as a premonition, or prophecy. A prophecy is often thought to be the ability to know or see something that will happen in the future. However, prophecies can be received for present time events. Through my dream, I received a psychic vision that prophesied Sally calling me to report the murder only a few hours before it actually happened.

While these dreams took place many years before being told, "You were scheduled to die, but the universe has changed," I was already receiving messages from the universe. I simply was not in that place in my life that I had learned to accept them. For many years, I worked hard to ignore my inner voice and visions. To be truthful, they scared me, and I did not want to openly discuss them for fear of other people's judgments. I thought I was doing something wrong. I still remembered my mother's premonitions of death and how we were not allowed to talk about them. Although she thought that she was protecting me, she was actually teaching me that having psychic experiences and communicating with spirits were not good things. I feel certain that it was due to her staunch religious upbringing.

We are all born with psychic senses. Young children exhibit these gifts because they are still uninhibited and have not yet been trained that if you cannot see something with your physical eyes, it is imaginary. It is very important that we allow our children to enjoy and develop their special gifts. We can learn a great deal from them. Adults think it is cute when a child talks to and plays with an imaginary friend. If those same adults would ask for more details of the child's playmate, they might discover that the invisible friend is actually a deceased family member. Stories abound where a small child describes, in great detail, talking with a deceased grandmother or grandfather about things that happened a decade or more before his or her birth.

Historically, science has taught that our senses are only physical. We see things with our eyes, feel things with our hands, hear voices with our ears, taste with our mouths, and smell with our noses. This is the way of science. It is measurable. If it cannot be seen or measured, it does not exist. It is as simple as that. Or is it?

The past few decades have witnessed new ways in which scientists are viewing our senses. These new viewpoints have developed primarily through the study of our brains in regard to our memories and dreams. The organ called the brain is essential to our life, but oddly enough, in spite of this space age in which we live, only a small portion of how the brain functions is understood. Scientists are now admitting that it is not clear how our memories are stored or how dreams occur. Some of these same scientists now believe that what we once thought to be our five physical senses of seeing, hearing, feeling, smelling, and touching are, in actuality, nine senses. They have recently included four additional psychic senses: the ability of seeing without the use of our eyes, hearing without audible sounds in our ears, feeling without actually touching an object, and knowing about something without having past experiences to provide that knowledge. These additional psychic senses are now referred to as clairvoyance, clairaudience, clairsentience, and claircognizance. Recently, a few laboratories testing psychic abilities have included clairalience, or the psychic sense of smell.

Clairvoyance is a French word meaning "clear seeing." Clairvoyant visions are most common in dreams or while meditating and differ only in how people have the experiences. A clairvoyant vision may happen externally, internally, or be combined with other psychic senses.

A friend of mine, who requested to remain anonymous, told a remarkable story of driving to her mother's house with her two children in the back seat. It was late at night, and the children had fallen asleep as she drove the narrow, desolate farm road. Without warning, she had a picture in her mind of a car crashing into her at a high speed. She had no idea of why she would have this vision. A tractor had been the only other vehicle she had seen for miles. She could only remember seeing herself swerve the car off of the road and into a cotton field to avoid the accident.

Within an hour, and only a short distance from the town where her mother lived, a pickup truck turned out of an intersecting road and was in her lane, speeding toward her head-on. Because of her clairvoyant warning, she turned the steering wheel sharply to the right and missed crashing with the truck. She believes that she and her daughters' lives were saved because of this clairvoyant vision.

Clairaudience is derived from the French word meaning "clear hearing." Have you ever clearly heard someone call your name, only to turn around and find no one there? If you have, you are not alone. The voice was probably as clear as if the unidentified person was standing ten feet away, but yet, no one is present. This is a prime example of clairaudience. With clairaudience, the voice heard is not that of your own inner voice, and it clearly belongs to another person or entity. The voice can be external and sound loud, as if it is coming from another room, across the street, or standing over you to awaken you from a deep sleep. It can also manifest as a low whisper.

The first time I remember experiencing clairaudience was when I was maybe nine or ten years old. I was walking to my elementary school and clearly heard my name called out. I stopped walking and turned to see if my mother was chasing after me for some reason. No one was there. The adult voice was very loud and clear as it called my name. I told myself that I had only imagined the voice, but deep down, I knew that the voice was real. Nevertheless, I kept to myself about hearing voices. My clairaudient ah-ha moment came when I was researching for this book and read *Black Elk Speaks*. Black Elk, an Oglala Sioux holy man born in 1863, was describing his life as a young boy and recalled the following:

> Maybe it was not this summer when I first heard the voices, but I think it was, because I know it was before I played with bows and arrows or rode a horse, and I was out playing alone when I heard them. It was like somebody calling me, and I thought it was my mother, but there was nobody there. This happened more than once, and always made me afraid, so that I ran home. [16]

The voices that Black Elk refers to were the sacred voices of the grandfathers preparing him for his holy life. Many religions may refer to this as "a calling." After learning of Black Elk's experiences, I felt somewhat

16 Neihardt, 18.

relieved that I was not imagining what I had heard as a child. I remember a few other occasions either on the playground or walking to or from school when I heard the voice calling to me. Finally, I assumed that whoever was talking to me gave up trying to communicate and went away. In hindsight, I wonder what might have happened had I actually responded to him and opened communication.

Clairsentience means "clear feeling," or is more commonly known as "gut feeling" or "intuition." Clairsentience often refers to the ability to feel vibrations of other people or places, and it can also assist in solving a problem you have been facing. How many times have you said something like, "I want to purchase that blue car, but my gut feeling is telling me to wait"? Or maybe you have had thoughts about someone only to run into that person a short time later. We have all had experiences like this. I, for one, have learned in recent years to listen to that gut feeling—that little voice inside that is screaming at me to do the right thing or to pick up the telephone and contact that long-lost friend.

In June 2005, I was on summer break from a high school across town where I was teaching English. I enjoyed being there, and although I would have preferred to teach reading, I was not looking for another position or school. On this particular morning, I woke up early as usual and quickly jumped out of bed. My husband, still half asleep asked, "What are you doing?"

"I've got to go update my resume," I replied in a very matter-of-fact tone, as if this was a normal thing to be doing at that time of the morning.

"Why? What for?" This made no sense to him, because he knew that I liked my job.

"I have to take my resume to Pirate Cove High School. I don't know why, but it's very important that they get it this morning." Even before I had opened my eyes, while I was still in that half-asleep and half-awake state, my inner voice was demanding that I do this. I felt an intense sense of urgency.

"All right. Do what you have to do," he said, rolling over and pulling the covers over his head. After years of being married to me, he knew that it would not do any good to pursue this any longer. I was on a mission.

Without knowing anything about the school or if they even had openings, I dropped off my resume at ten o'clock that morning. At eleven thirty, the school's secretary called to schedule an interview for the following morning. This alone was the first validation I needed that my inner voice had given me proper guidance. The second validation came during the interview when I was, on the spot, offered a position to teach *reading*. The universe works in wonderful and mysterious ways!

I cannot recall a single time when I have been misguided by those inner messages. However, as I look back at my life, I can accurately say that in *every* situation where I did not listen to my gut feeling, the action resulted in disaster. Every time!

Lynn B. Robinson, PhD, author of *Coming Out Of Your Psychic Closet: How to Unlock Your Naturally Intuitive Self*, is a long-time friend and one of my former University of South Alabama professors. She expertly explains that while intuition is both a natural and normal part of all of us, most of us are too embarrassed or ashamed to admit having these experiences and live our lives locked in a psychic closet. In her book, she offers ways of discovering your own personal intuitiveness, as well as methods for validating and strengthening your psychic, intuitive self.

Claircognizance very simply means "clear knowing." We realize that we know things with no reasonable explanation for how we know what we know. We just do. An example of this "just knowing" involved my receiving a grape vine as a gift several years ago. I knew absolutely nothing about growing them except that they made beautiful vines that could cover an arbor or trellis. It never occurred to me to purchase a trellis at the local garden center; however, I knew that it was my mission to construct my own grape arbor. I am not a carpenter, and I have never built anything like this before or since. But, in this situation, I instinctively knew what to do and proceeded to work. I cut bamboo stalks from a far corner of the yard and hauled them around to the southern-most side of my house where the grapes could benefit from the most direct sunlight. I began laying out the vertical stalks and measured for the horizontal poles and cross braces. Using jute rope, I tied all of the stalks together and ended with an absolutely amazing grape arbor. When I stood back and looked at it—especially after the grapevine had covered it, and my first tiny grapes were hanging gracefully—I had absolutely no idea as to how I had built it. Even more amazing was that was the year we had a series of hurricanes move through our area. Although there was considerable tree damage and flooding, my little grape arbor remained standing, even though the privacy fence behind it was lying on the ground.

Clairalience, or "clear smelling," is a psychic way of receiving smells, emotions, and other physical senses giving way to psychic impressions. There are endless lists of stories about families reporting smells associated with deceased family members. These accounts might include the smell of a specific pipe tobacco enjoyed by Grandpa, the beautiful aroma of roses that Great-Grandmother always kept in her living room, the comforting smell of fresh bread baking when there is no one baking in the house, etc. I'm certain that if you think about it, you will also remember a time when a touch, smell, or taste immediately reminded you of a lost loved one or another very special time in your life. *Clairgustance* is a psychic sense meaning "clear taste." Those who experience clairgustance become receptive to messages from the spiritual or ethereal realms through taste.

Psychometry is generally related to both clairvoyance and clairsentience but may incorporate any of the above mentioned "clairs." Psychometry, through touch alone, enables a person to sense or experience psychic impressions surrounding the history of an object or clairvoyantly gain knowledge about the past or present life of the person associated with the item. Psychic investigators use psychometry to assist police in solving crimes. These psychics or mediums hold items belonging to the victims and receive psychic impressions about the victim and the crime. In many cases, the psychics are able to see and feel the crime as it happened due to residual energy contained in the object being held. Television drama also highlights shows such as *The Dead Zone* based on Steven Spielberg's novel by the same name. In the show, Johnny Smith awakens from a coma and finds that he has amazing psychic powers to see into both past and future. His visions are psychometric and triggered by touch.

Until recently, I could only grasp the concept of psychometry and thought that I knew what it is and how it works. My friend Pam and I participated in a day-long workshop presented by Dr. Brian Weiss, author of many best-selling books, including *Many Lives Many Masters*. Dr. Weiss is a psychotherapist whose professional life was completely altered when one of his patients began relaying information about her past lives—actions that, as a scientist, he had been trained not to believe. His viewpoint of past lives changed when this same patient began to channel information to him about his own family and deceased son.

Fourteen hundred people were in attendance at the Ft. Lauderdale, Florida, workshop. The first thing I noticed was the intense energy that could be felt in the huge conference room. The collective energies of that many people all thinking and feeling the same thing at the same time is extremely powerful. During the afternoon session, Dr. Weiss announced that we were going to do an exercise in psychometry and asked that we exchange something personal with someone sitting next to us. Pam handed me one of her rings. The lights dimmed, and Dr. Weiss talked us through a guided meditation focusing on the object we were holding. As I sat holding Pam's ring, eyes closed, listening to Dr. Weiss's soothing voice, an image of a little girl popped into my vision. She was probably about four years old and had dark, sandy-colored hair. She seemed to just pop in, smile at me, and then pop out. This happened at least three times during the short meditation. When we were brought out of our meditative trance, I turned and looked at Pam.

"Well?" she inquired. "Did you see anything?"

"Oh, yes. I certainly did," I replied.

"What? Stop with the suspense!"

I took a deep breath and proceeded. "I saw a little girl."

"What did she look like?" she questioned.

I described the little girl as best I could.

"Was she my granddaughter?"

"No, I'm almost certain this was a different little girl."

"Oh my God!" she shrieked as if she had just remembered something very important.

"What?" It was my turn to ask questions.

"A medium at Cassadaga told me about seeing a little girl when we were there several years ago. He said that she was just bouncing all over the place."

"Pam, you never told me about that," I scolded her.

"No, I didn't. I just wanted to see what would happen."

"And now you know," I said laughingly. "She is obviously still running around you."

"I wonder who she is," she questioned.

"Or … who she was." We both laughed as this bit of past life humor.

Since the seminar, Pam has spent many hours going through old family photos and has yet to determine who the little girl might be.

For me, this was my own personal validation of the power of psychometry. There was no doubt that I saw this little girl. Her appearance was much like watching a short television commercial. The vision was in full, living color, and she was vibrant, happy, and seemed to be full of life. If I were able to experience this during my first attempt with psychometry, I could not help to wonder what it must be like for certified mediums who deal with this on a daily basis.

Overview

- Déjà vu is a feeling of either having been somewhere before or a familiar sense of having met or seen a complete stranger somewhere in the past.
- Dreams can be a form of psychic vision.
- We are all born with psychic senses.
- The brain is an essential life organ. Science understands only a small portion of how it functions. It is not clear how our memories are stored or how dreams occur.
- Clairvoyance is a psychic sense meaning "clear seeing." It is most common to happen while dreaming or meditating but has also been documented to occur while the person is wide awake.
- Clairaudience is a psychic sense meaning "clear hearing." The voice heard is not your own inner voice and clearly belongs to another person or entity.
- Clairsentience is a psychic sense meaning "clear feeling." It is more commonly known as gut feeling or intuition.
- Claircognizance is a psychic sense meaning "clear knowing." It is a realization that you know something with no reasonable explanation for how or why. You just do.
- Clairalience is a psychic sense meaning "clear smelling." Clairalience enables you to detect smells, emotions, and other physical senses, giving way to psychic impressions.
- Clairgustance is a psychic sense meaning "clear taste." Those who experience clairgustance become receptive to messages from spiritual or ethereal realms through taste.
- Psychometry is a psychic sense that enables a person to sense or experience psychic impressions surrounding the history of an object or clairvoyantly gain knowledge about the past or present life of the person associated with the item through touch alone.

<u>Your Psychic Journal:</u>

It is time for you to reflect once again upon your own life. You have just read about several psychic senses that many scientists now acknowledge.

- Was there a time in your life when you experienced even one of these senses? What happened? Remember to include details.
- Have you ever been in a situation and suddenly realized (or thought for a brief moment) that you had dreamed being there before?

Be honest with yourself in remembering any and all of these events. Write them down even if you want to say that it happened due to a coincidence. This is your time of discovery.

Think, reflect, and happy journaling!

Chapter Eleven

Spiritualism: Mediums and Myths

Howbeit when he, the Spirit of truth, is come,
he will guide you into all truth: for he shall not speak of himself;
but whatsoever he shall hear, that shall he speak:
and he will shew you things to come.
John 16:13

You have only to turn on the television almost any day of the week to find programs dealing with mediums, ghost hunters, and other paranormal phenomena. *John Edward Cross Country*, *Medium*, *Ghost Whisperer*, *The Dead Zone*, *Psychic Children*, *Psychic Detectives*, *Ghost Hunters*, *Ghost Adventures*, *Paranormal State*, *Haunted History*, and *Ghost Hunters International* are only a few examples. Mediums such as James Van Praagh, Sylvia Browne, John Holland, Allison Dubois, and many other names have become commonplace discussion in our society. Never before in our country's history have so many people become interested in Spiritualism and the paranormal.

Before we discuss what spiritualism and mediumship are, we should talk about what they are not. True spiritualists and mediums are not fortune tellers. They are not, as some people still want to believe, conducting the work of the devil, because they communicate with the dead. I never cease to be amazed by questions I receive when I mention that I am going on a spiritual retreat.

- Are you going to have your fortune read?
- Does your fortune teller use a crystal ball?
- Can you have a curse put on someone for me?
- Can you get a curse removed from me?
- Do you have your own Ouija board?

I usually respond with something equally as intelligent, such as, "And I will not be flying my broom to the retreat this time." This generally quiets them while they ponder whether I am teasing.

Spiritualism is a religion. Spiritualist churches can be found in most of America's communities and have strong followings throughout Europe and many other countries around the world. Concepts from all major world religions and theosophy, or divine mystical wisdom, are integral in its teachings.

"Spiritualists believe that the human being is a spirit and is therefore a part of God; in the continuity of life; and in each individual's responsibility to make his own happiness or unhappiness as he obeys Nature's physical and spiritual laws. They live their lives by the belief that the highest morality is written in the Golden Rule: Whatsoever that ye would that others should do unto you, do ye also unto them."[17] A true spiritualist or medium will never sit for a reading without first asking for divine protection and guidance.

Spiritualism is also a science and a philosophy. As a science, Spiritualism investigates spirit phenomena and then places them into classifications. Philosophically, spiritualism studies the laws of both spirit and physical worlds. One spiritualist principle affirms that communication with the so-called dead is a fact, scientifically proven by the phenomenon of Spiritualism. Spiritualists maintain that it has been proven through mediumship and parapsychology that mediums are able to gain information using channels other than the traditional five senses. It is important to note that not all spiritualists are mediums or healers; and likewise, not all mediums are spiritualists.

An important myth to be discussed is the fact that Spiritualism is not witchcraft. I find it difficult to believe that in our cyberspace age of knowledge, many still confuse the two and carry forward ideas and biases derived from ancient Puritanical beliefs. Queen Elizabeth I, in 1563, passed England's most notorious Witchcraft Act. The Church of England declared that everyone would live by its laws and beliefs. This misguided concept led to many innocent people being burned at the stake

17 Cassadaga, 7.

as witches. Later, George II passed the Witchcraft Act of 1735. This new act only somewhat reversed the earlier misconceptions. It declared that anyone pretending to have spiritual powers to summon spirits would no longer be burned or hanged but instead would be considered as a vagrant or con artist and would face penalties of fines and/or imprisonment. Many years later the Fraudulent Mediums Act of 1951 was enacted. It prohibited anyone from claiming to be a medium or other Spiritualist for the purpose of making money via deception. Mediumship was to be used for entertainment purposes only. This act was at last replaced in 2008 by new Consumer Protection Regulations, which targeted unfair marketing and sales practices.

It is unfortunate that there remain so many people who do not have a clear understanding of the differences. I am even more surprised at how many associate something dark, demonic, sinister, or even evil with the mere mention of the word medium or spirit. Please understand that I have attempted to clarify that Spiritualism and witchcraft are different entities. At the same time, in no way do I intend to imply that witchcraft, or Wicca, is to be considered evil. "Wicca, as the Old Craft, is a religion that teaches connections to Nature and more importantly to the forces behind Nature.… The Craft is a system of spiritual development … everything connects and shares a relationship with everything else. What we do to the Earth, and to each other, we do to ourselves."[18] These are Wiccan beliefs, and I, for one, see nothing sinister. Do you? And guess what else? They don't ride around on broomsticks either! Pure myth!

Throughout history, mediums have been known by many names, such as oracles, soothsayers, shamans, mystics, prophets, channelers, witches, wizards, medicine men, and sorcerers. A medium has proven capabilities of communicating with spirits through various forms of phenomena.[19] They act as channels of information between the spirit and Earth planes. My own research has led me to believe that there is a very fine line between a medium and what we now interchangeably call a psychic. I understand mediums to be those who act as direct links between the living and the spirit world. Psychics, on the other hand, are able to see into the past or

18 Raven Grimassi, *Wiccan Magick: Inner Teachings of the Craft* (St. Paul: Llewellyn Publications, 1998), 4–5.

19 The term "phenomena" is used to describe a wide variety of manifestations and Spirit communications which may include: clairvoyance, clairaudience, clairsentience, claircognizance; clairalience; psychometry; healing; levitation, materialization, trances, and automatic writing/drawing/painting.

future by tapping into energies. Not all mediums are psychics, and not all psychics are mediums.

Definitions of both indicate that the *gift* either manifests itself early in childhood or may begin later in adult years as the result of a near death experience, trauma to the head, or severe grief. Mediumship generally manifests as being mental or physical. In mental mediumship, the medium generally taps into the spirit world either through the use of one or more of the five "clairs" mentioned earlier or by automatic writing or trance speech. Physical mediums are more prone to use levitation, rappings, table tipping, and the moving of objects. Mediums today are generally more mental than physical, although physical mediumship is practiced. I do not understand why this is, other than fraudulent practices were more commonplace within physical mediumship in the early history of spiritualism.

In those early days, many so-called physical mediums became magicians on stage in order to earn incomes by performing their magic. There are physical mediums today who allow spirits to enter their bodies and speak through them. This type of spirit communication is referred to as a "step in." You may be familiar with the movie *Ghost*. Patrick Swayze performed a step in by using Whoopi Goldberg's character to communicate with Demi Moore.

There are probably as many reasons to consult a medium as there are for going to any other type of counselor. While some may be seeking information about jobs, family, career, finances, or health, others may actually be looking for closure to the death of a loved one. They are more than likely wanting to know if their loved ones are without pain. Are they happy? Have they seen other family members or pets who have passed? Will they win the lottery? Will these truth-seekers receive answers to their questions? Maybe and maybe not.

Shopper, beware! Certified mediums are not one size fits all. While you might conduct an Internet search to find a medium, and there are thousands on the Internet, you should—and must—do your homework to make certain that you will be selecting one who is genuine and certified. If a fortune teller is what you are seeking, then run to the first door you see that has a psychic readings sign hanging over it. Sometimes, you might even find a reader sitting at a card table on a sidewalk somewhere, and for five or ten dollars they will tell you a few generic things that they have memorized and tell everyone they see. I also hear horror stories of people spending their entire life's savings making telephone or Internet calls to psychics. Sadly, most of those making the calls are already in a desperate financial or personal situation, and the astronomical amount of money it costs for these "per-minute consultations" makes the situation even worse.

So how does one locate a true medium? As with any other professional service, you do your research. Find out all you can about the medium's credentials and reputation. Word-of-mouth referrals from trusted friends or associates are always safe. New Age bookstores are also another great resource, not only for locating mediums but also information for classes such as yoga, meditation, and Tai Chi, as well as listings of upcoming speakers and/or spiritual workshops. If you are fortunate enough to have a spiritualist community in your area, by all means go and visit. Cassadaga Spiritualist Camp, as I have mentioned throughout this book, is where I choose to go for my mindfulness retreats. At least once a year, the camp sponsors a psychic fair. It is during this activity-filled day that newcomers, curiosity seekers, and many of us old-timers, are given the opportunity to "try on" different mediums who offer minireadings for only a few dollars a sitting.

Fees vary from location to location and can be dependent upon variables, such as the length of time you select for a reading. For example, a thirty-minute reading is obviously not as costly as for a full hour. There are also differences in fees based upon the reputation of the medium. As with office charges for a general family practitioner versus those of a highly skilled surgeon, medium rates vary greatly between those of a local bookstore medium as compared to what is charged by an internationally recognized medium with best-seller books to his acclaim. Fees or rates should be agreed upon in advance of the reading. A request for additional money, during or after a reading, is cause for concern and should be reported.

It is important that you select a medium with whom you connect spiritually and that the medium is likewise able to connect with you. I cannot tell you how you will know when that connection happens—you just will. On our first visit to Cassadaga, Pam and I were still in the "shopping" mode. At that time, we actually had no idea of what we were seeking—or what we were doing for that matter. Together, we selected a name from the sign-in board in the camp bookstore, telephoned for an appointment, and walked to his house. As we walked, we agreed that whichever one of us he gravitated toward would have the first reading.

I remember him walking through the front door and grabbing my hand while saying, "You're the one I spoke with on the phone, aren't you?

I need to see you immediately. I heard something in your voice when you called, and we need to talk now." We were both startled by this obvious sense of emergency. He looked at Pam and suggested, very apologetically, that she wait outside in his sunroom while he read for me. It turned out that my reading was totally unbelievable. He told me specific details about my entire life, and I had never seen this man before. While Pam had been studying past life regressions, I had not, but it didn't stop him from explaining that the room was completely filled with spirits from my former lives. He explained that this had never happened before during a first reading. He also gave me some good advice about my upcoming future, which, as it turns out, actually went the way he described. He also cautioned me to be alert to health issues. He was concerned about blood pressure or something dealing with blood. (Hmmm? Could it have been my forthcoming brain bleed?) I took pages of notes, which I still refer to even after all these years. By the time my session ended and I finally walked back outside to see Pam, I was beaming with excitement.

We had a few minutes to talk while he prepared for her reading, and my excitement rubbed off on her. She could not wait to be called in. You have probably already guessed the outcome. Her reading was disastrous. There didn't seem to be any connection between them, spiritual or otherwise. Pam, still to this day, accuses me of using up all of his energies so that there was nothing left for her. That could have well been the case, but one thing is certain—he remained my advisor for the next six years. Pam had to try out a few more before finding her comfort zone.

By the way, most mediums will allow you to record during readings, and many will make the tapes or CDs available for a dollar or two. I highly recommend this, because so much information is given in a short period of time. Unless your memory is much better than mine, it is helpful to have the session recorded and be able to play it back at a later date. I always hear things during the playback that I missed hearing during the initial reading. Mediums vocalize the information as they receive it, and trust me, it comes at a fast pace.

In preparing for a reading, relax your mind and body before the meeting. It is important to be open and receptive to receiving your messages. I have found that prayer and meditation work for me. I always concentrate on releasing any negative energy I have prior to the reading. I pray that I accept only positive energies and that I will not be affected by any negatives that I may encounter. If I have any specific questions that I would like answered, I focus on those questions during the meditation.

If possible, I try to sit alone in meditation for fifteen to twenty minutes prior to a reading.

Once the reading has begun, allow the medium to proceed at his own pace. Do not provide too much information in the beginning. Let him know when correct information has been communicated, and do not argue if a message comes through that you do not agree with. Some information may make more sense to you by the end of the reading, while other information may not become clear until a much later date when you have had a chance to think about it. There have been many times when I have had another ah-ha moment after something happens, and I remember that it was contained in a reading from months before. A successful reading is not measured by the message or prophecy, but by the guidance it provides for harmonious living. Above all, do not expect that all of your questions will be answered at once. The medium will ask you near the end of the reading if you have any specific questions. I have generally found that those questions that I included in my preparatory meditation are answered during the reading, leaving me with very little to ask.

You should not have a reading too frequently and then only if there is a sincere need. Once every six months or longer is preferred. I was recently told a story of someone living near me who will not make any life decisions without first speaking with a medium. This is not healthy no matter how you look at it—not to mention that it would be very costly. Please do not go to a reading so that you can decide what to wear to cousin Bessie's wedding, which color car you should purchase, or whether you should purchase single- or two-ply toilet tissue. Mediums are professionals and should be regarded as such. Use their services as you would any other professional.

I am convinced there is a reason that certain people enter our lives at different times and for different purposes. So it is with mediums. During my early experiences and growth, I was very comfortable going back to my first medium every six months. Then, as I mentioned earlier in chapter three, my longtime advisor told me that I no longer needed to have him read for me, and I became quite concerned as to why he had told me that. The ego is our enemy and likes to control with fear, and so it was with me. I wondered if I had done something wrong, when I had not. The universe was simply preparing me for the next part of my journey.

Within six months, Rev. Don Zanghi entered my life with the force of March winds. As described in chapter three, his spirit guide, Dr. Huxley, delivered a life-altering message to me. At the time, this did not seem like an appropriate message for Don to relay, but he did. Seven months later, I was in the hospital undergoing my brain surgeries. My doctors and nurses all told me that I was their miracle patient. The true miracle here was that I never, at any time, worried that I would not survive. I *knew* that although I had been scheduled to die, the universe had changed. I *knew* that I would continue life with a renewed purpose and perspective. Don and I have now become friends, and due to the doctor's message, we realize that we have a highly spiritual bond. He has confided in me that he now tells my/our story in many of his lectures and seminars.

A few years ago, I was inspired to write a letter to a well-known medium, who I discovered lives in my area. I had never done anything like it before, but once again, I listened to that inner voice that screamed to me saying, *Write the letter.* With great delight, Lydia Clar answered me. She is a highly respected, lifelong medium in her own right, and in more recent years, she has been given credit as the first medium to read psychic John Edward. I now respectively consider Lydia not only my teacher but also my friend. Lydia's new book, *Out Of Darkness Into Light: My Personal Journey into the Realm of Spirit*, is now available. She describes how her psychic career began and also discusses how to trust the messages and guidance sent to you from the spirit realm. Lydia believes that everyone has psychic abilities waiting to be tapped.

The universe is a wonderful place!

Overview

- Never before in our country's history have so many people become interested in Spiritualism and the paranormal.
- Spiritualism is classified as a religion, a science, and a philosophy. Concepts from all major world religions and theosophy, or divine mystical wisdom, are integral in its teachings.
- Mediums act as direct links between the living and the spirit world; psychics are able to see into the past and the future by tapping into energies of both the living and dead.
- Not all mediums are psychics, and not all psychics are mediums.
- Caution should be taken when selecting a reader. There are many fraudulent people claiming to be psychics or mediums. Get reliable referrals from trusted sources before scheduling a reading.

- Arrange the fee in advance of the reading.
- Take a recorder to your session or arrange to have the reading recorded for later playback.
- Allow the reader to proceed at his or her pace. Do not offer too much information in the beginning.
- Do not argue if the reader says something that you disagree with. It may make sense much later.
- Save any specific questions you have until the end of the session. In most cases, your questions will be answered during the reading.

Your Psychic Journal:

Congratulations! You have once again arrived at that place where you open your mind and journal to enter new observations, memories, or thoughts.

- What experiences have you had with a psychic or medium?
- Now that you are aware of how personal energies interact, do you remember a reading when your energy and that of the medium complemented each other?
- Have you experienced a bad reading because your energies were in opposition to each other?
- How did you locate the medium you selected?
- How valid was the message you received?
- Have you ever delivered a psychic message to another person?

You should use your psychic journal to log information received during each psychic reading. This makes the journal a useful tool that you can turn to after an event occurs weeks or even months after the reading. That surprising, unplanned ah-ha moment when you say, "I think I was told about this in a reading I had a few months ago" that becomes validation.

Think, reflect, and happy journaling!

Chapter Twelve

The Mysterious World of Orbs

"Look how the floor of heaven
Is thick inlaid with patines of bright gold:
There's not the smallest orb which thou behold'st
But in his motion like an angel sings. . . ."
Shakespeare, The Merchant of Venice

I will always remember June 14, 2007 as the date when I had my first encounter with orbs, small balls of light and energy that seem to interact and communicate with an intuitive intelligence. Most orbs cannot be seen with the human eye but appear to be readily visible through the lens of a digital camera. As with my research about the universe and as difficult as it might be to believe, I was not the first person to have an orb experience. In fact, these small light forms have fascinated people since the dawn of civilization. Drawings, carvings, and etchings created by our early ancestors generally include some form of circular, orb-like entities. Most religious artworks, both past and present, contain purposely positioned orbs or circular symbols. Jesus, saints, and angels are depicted with glowing orbs of light that we recognize as halos. Orbs have always played an important role for Native Americans, who believe that everything in life moves in a circle.

It would appear that orb hunting has become a worldwide pastime, because so many people are reporting encounters and photographing these mysterious luminosities. Scottish photographer Ian Cameron (www.transientlight.co.uk/index.php) coined the term transient light to mean the special moment when light, its color, strength, and direction transform a scene from the ordinary to the extraordinary. In their book *Beyond Photography*, Katie Hall and John Pickering described the lights they photographed at their home in England as small transient lights (STLs). So what are they? Where do they come from?

Over time, I have taken what may be thousands of pictures and had never photographed an orb, and then seemingly, without reason, they began to appear. Are they the result of the conscious mind, spirit manifestations, or camera malfunctions, or are they the result of external impediments such as dust, water droplets, insects, etc., as some skeptics want you to believe? While orbs have been witnessed since the early days of humanity, they seem to be appearing more now than ever before. Are they making their presence known to us more now than in the past, or is it because most amateur photographers are now using digital cameras, which seem to capture them more frequently? Might it be a combination of both?

From a scientific point of view, every orb can be explained with very few exceptions. Those few exceptions, according to modern scientists, are referred to as "naturally occurring phenomenon." In other words, if it occurs naturally, it is not a spiritual or paranormal phenomenon. I might have easily accepted this rationality had I not personally experienced the orbs myself. I know that what I saw and felt was real.

During the course of my research, I discovered others who are convinced that these balls of light do, in fact, exist. Unfortunately, most of those believers are not scientists, and therefore, what they say and have experienced offers no more scientific credibility than what I have to offer. But one fact remains constant: those of us who have witnessed these luminosities know that they are real. There were a few times during this writing when I was reminded of an article about someone in Wyoming or Oregon who claimed to have been kidnapped by aliens. Generally, many of us chuckle and guffaw at claims of UFO abductions. Now that I have had my own paranormal and spiritual experiences, I look at those stories with a new perspective. If we have not walked in another's shoes, we cannot confirm or deny his experiences as being anything but real—scientifically proven or not.

In March 2001, Lenore Sweet, PhD, noticed mysterious light forms in two photographs she had taken. This first encounter was the catalyst launching her and her brother Peter on an incredible journey photographing light anomalies. *How To Photograph The Paranormal* was at first to be a book describing what these luminosities are. However, like me and many others, she soon became aware that no matter how long the search, she may never be able to say without a doubt what or who they are. She then decided her goal was to write a book that would examine paranormal light theories and provide instruction for photographing orbs.

Beyond Photography follows the remarkable journey of Hall and Pickering, beginning in April 2002. It was at this time, while they were photographing a woodland area near their nineteenth-century English home that orbs began to appear in their photographs. Within a short time period, they noticed that the orbs were multiplying in number, and at the same time, they began photographing other light forms in the shape of rods, vapors, vortexes, and winged apparitions. They discovered that, in many situations, the luminosities seemed to interact with them and at times responded to their vocal commands. In my opinion, *Beyond Photography* is the most complete, in-depth, and unbiased study of orbs currently available.

The above mentioned authors agree that these light forms, whatever they are, are intelligent and do communicate and interact with our human world. At times, the forms appear to materialize due to our conscious thoughts. That could explain their appearance in Cassadaga on June 14, 2007. On that night, we had six people together all holding the same intentions of having a visual experience, and it happened. Could this be the power of collective consciousness at work?

Let us first take a look at some current debunking ideas regarding photographing orbs with digital cameras. While digitals appear to be capturing more orbs and other luminosities than the older 35 mm cameras, they also are better at photographing dust, mist, and insects. We know that recent improvements in digital technology provide us with much higher-quality pictures. At the same time, these technological improvements have produced a new generation of cameras capable of capturing tiny airborne particles previously missed with older technologies, including our eyes.

My friend Pam took the following picture of a hospital nursery as it was nearing completion. (Figure 12.1) Take a close look at it. What do you think? Are these orbs or airborne particles?

Photograph by Pamela S. Bridges
Figure 12.1 Hospital Nursery Orbs

If you answered dust particles, you are *probably* right. While the hospital took every measure to contain dust during construction, you and I both know that it is going to happen anyway. Pam insists that on the day she took this photograph, she personally could not see signs of anything airborne. However, the simple fact that this is a construction site leads us to believe that what we are seeing are not orbs—at least, not all of them.

Technology has made cameras smaller, and along with the reduced size, the distance between the lens and flash has decreased. When this happens, the light angle leading to the lens increases the possibility of light reflection off of what would normally be invisible dust particles. These orb imposters may result from not only dust, but water droplets, mist, fingerprints, or any other foreign material that settles on the lens. This lends great credibility to the belief that most so-called orbs are anomalies that have been captured by the camera and are not paranormal phenomena.

On the other hand, many people believe in reincarnation of the soul. Their beliefs assert that a soul may appear in the form of an orb during its transition into the afterlife and that it may also be seen as an orb just prior to its rebirth, the time when the soul enters the body. For example, let us reexamine Figure 12.1 from the perspective of Tibetan Buddhism, which believes that the soul is eternal; it is born into the light, dies into the light, and is reborn into the light. This religion teaches that there are three distinct stages of death, or bardo, which take forty-nine days to complete.

- Stage one, Chikai Bardo. This is the actual process of dying when the spirit leaves the physical body and moves into the light.
- Stage two, Chonyid Bardo. A spirit Buddhist monk, a Lama, reviews the deceased's life with the soul and grants one white pebble for each good deed and one black pebble for each bad deed. The result of this judgment determines the soul's pathway in the final stage.
- Stage three, Sidpa Bardo. It is during this third stage that the conscious soul, assuming it lived a good life (more white pebbles), has the opportunity to select new parents and return to the physical world. A reincarnating soul returns to the physical realm and remains close to its new parents while it awaits rebirth.

Now, look at Figure 12.1 again. Overlooking the fact that this hospital nursery is under construction with every effort made to eliminate dust, is it possible that a few of these orbs may be souls waiting to reincarnate? *It's possible.*

Recently, I had an appointment to have my hair done. My hairdresser, aware that I was writing this book, was eager to show me a picture she had taken of her grown son. He was lying on her living room floor watching television. A perfectly formed orb hovered just to the top-right side of his head. She first wanted confirmation from me that this was, in fact, an orb; second, she asked me if I thought this might be the soul of his deceased father, her late husband. During our conversation, she happened to mention that he was about to become a new father. *Here was another of my ah-ha moments. This orb was possibly the reincarnating soul of his soon-to-be child, or it may have also been the protective spirit of his late father. I do not know. The one thing I am aware of is the fact that orbs appear everywhere in the world and to people of all walks of life and ages.*

Many of my students, aware of my orb investigations, have brought in pictures that they have taken of orbs. Some appear in their bedrooms at night, others show up in church during services, while still others appear in their cars as they are traveling. One of my female students told me that she has had orbs around her for her entire life. Many of her childhood pictures in their family album show her surrounded by mystical balls of light.

In chapter four, I described a mild electrical shock from an orb when I passed my hand through the space it occupied. While it was not the most intelligent thing I had ever done, it taught me that orbs contain energy—enough to provide a jolt to humans. That particular orb had three distinct characteristics: it was completely visible to the naked eye, it contained a noticeable amount of charged energy, and it radiated an intuitive feeling of intelligence. I did not require scientific verification to convince me that I had just received shock therapy administered by my small, yellow orb friend. I saw what I saw, and I felt what I felt.

Its first characteristic was remarkable in that its shape and color were clearly visible. Second, to have received the shock was totally amazing! Together, these two characteristics of orbs are thought to be, in some scientific circles, an anomaly called ball lightning. This phenomenon, which normally accompanies electrical storms, has been documented by thousands of people around the world. It has been described to range anywhere from the size of a tennis ball to that of a basketball. A lightning ball may appear suddenly, skip across a floor, and bounce around in a room before exploding in a flash of light. Ball lightning has a bright glow that is comparable to a one hundred-watt lightbulb. Some scientists believe that ball lightning is a plasma cloud created by lightning-charged atoms. When enough charged atoms are present, the electromagnetic energy sets off a visible fluorescent light. This, again, is a theory but a substantial one that might be applied to at least some orb reports. I do not believe that my shock was equivalent to what I would receive if I touched the bare wires of a one hundred-watt bulb powered by 110 volts. However, if the orb had been drawing from a lower energy source than lightning, such as human energy, it would then stand to reason that a dimmer fluorescent glow could be observed. It is also conceivable that it might contain enough energy to be felt by any human silly enough to reach out and touch it.

The orb's third characteristic, which I intuitively identified, was its intelligence. How could I sense this? How does anyone intuitively know anything? Scientists acknowledge that the universe, visible and invisible, is filled with vibrational energies known as electromagnetic energy (EME) frequencies. Intuition happens when our conscious minds act as information receivers and pick up on information carried by these EME frequencies. *Most adults, although they are born with these receivers, need training and practice to develop their intuitive skills.* Results of brain wave testing during the past few decades suggest that our conscious minds may send and receive signals much like those that transmit broadcast signals to our televisions, radios, and cellular telephones. Thank goodness that our mental frequencies operate at a much higher frequency than, say, those of an FM radio station. If they did not, everyone would be able to tune in and listen to each of our conscious thoughts!

Skeptics of this receiver theory argue that if our brains are so sensitive to EME frequencies, we should develop serious physical problems each time we come into contact with highly charged electrical fields. Thank goodness these skeptics are wrong. We are naturally protected from the *normal range* of daily EME frequencies we encounter. Physical illnesses cannot happen to us because we are protected by our skin, skull, and cerebrospinal fluids—our internal grounding system. However, we are all wired differently. Some are more sensitive to these frequencies than others. Remember the "clairs" (clairvoyance, clairsentience, clairaudience, clairalience, and claircognizance) from chapter ten? Each of these is received by way of this EME reception. Some people tend to be more receptive to sounds (inner voices), while others are more adapted to receive pictures (visions). This theory also explains why mediums and psychics are able to receive and deliver messages gathered from the universe.

NOTE: While you are internally protected from normal daily EME frequencies, you should never enter areas with extremely high EME readings without proper protective clothing. Examples of these locations are radio transmission stations, communication towers, and building rooftops serving as electronic communication sites. Never stand in front of a powerful transmitting antenna dish. These are dangerous areas, which can and will produce severe physical ailments following prolonged exposures. There is good reason why these sites all have danger and warning signs posted at the entrances.

Photograph by Robert G. Henderson
Figure 12.2 Orb over Isles of Capri, Florida

The above picture was taken while Pam and her husband were vacationing on Florida's gulf coast with friends. (Figure 12.2) This was a beautiful fall evening with no sign of thunderstorms in the area. At first glance, you can see the setting sun and a very full moon. However, there was no full moon on that particular night. This was a night of a very thin, waxing crescent moon. This orb mysteriously made its appearance and then vanished. Pam confirmed that the pictures taken before and after this one show only the remnants of the sunset—no sun, no orb, no full moon. In addition, there appears to be no explanation that might directly link this orb to the ball lightning or plasma cloud theories.

Another belief, which I have read in numerous books and publications, is that orbs may, in fact, be angels. By appearing in the photographs we take, they are letting us know that they are near. It is their way of telling us that we are not alone and reminding us that they are ever present to help, counsel, guide, and protect us. Our ancient ancestors did not have the instant technology that is at our disposal today. It makes sense that our digital orb photographs are simply more updated versions of our ancestors' carvings and drawings. These angel lights have been around throughout eternity, and we now have the technological means to capture their beauty.

As I look back to the night of June 14, I wonder if my orb friend was delivering an angelic message to me that something was wrong on that side of my head. Both its physical location and the resulting shock were, in fact, at the exact location of my brain bleed. Skeptics and naysayers might say that the electrical shock is probably what caused it in the first place. I do not believe this to be true, and neither does my neurosurgeon. The CAT scan and MRI reports revealed that I had suffered several bleeds and that it had been occurring over a longer period of time. It might also be that without the electrical shock, the bleeding may have been much more severe. *I might not be sitting here telling you this story.*

Overview

- Orbs, small circular light forms, have fascinated people since the beginning of time.
- Technological improvements have produced a new generation of digital cameras capable of capturing tiny airborne particles previously missed with older technologies, including our eyes. It is speculated that some 95 percent of reported orb pictures

are actually images of dust particles, water droplets, insects, or other materials that have settled on the camera's lens.

- Some scientists contend that an orb is an anomaly called ball lightning or a plasma cloud.
- A belief in reincarnation asserts that a soul may appear in the form of an orb during its transition into the afterlife and that it may also be seen as an orb just prior to its rebirth—the time when the soul enters the body.
- Orbs can interact with humans through intuition using electromagnetic frequencies.
- Practitioners of angelology and others believe that many orbs are angels. By appearing to us, they are reminding us that they are ever present to help, counsel, guide, and protect us.
- No one is able to say for certain what these small, translucent lights are. They have appeared throughout history of mankind, and today, orb hunting has become a photographic hobby for many.

Your Psychic Journal:

It is, once again, time for you to grab a pen and make a journal entry or two. Here are a couple of questions to help get you started.

- Have you or someone you know ever had an orb encounter? Describe the encounter. Who or what do you think the orb may have been?
- Have you ever taken a picture and had a strange light form appear with no plausible explanation? Describe the occasion.

Think, reflect, and happy journaling!

Chapter Thirteen

Angels

"Angels are spirits, but it is not because they are spirits that they are angels. They become angels when they are sent …
the name angel refers to their office, not their nature.
You ask the name of this nature, it is spirit;
you ask its office, it is Angel, which is a messenger."
Saint Augustine

"There are nine orders of angels … archangels, virtues, powers, principalities, dominions, thrones, cherubim, and seraphim."
Pope Gregory the Great

I have always believed in angels. It is a blessing that I have had for my entire life. Since I was old enough to sit in church and look at the beautiful statues and portraits of these heavenly bodies, I always knew that they existed. I never felt alone, even if there was no one else around. As a small child, I loved to run and play in the woods or forests, and it was during these times when I was most in touch with my invisible friends. I know it worried my mother when I would seemingly just disappear from her sight, even at two years of age, but for me, being alone in nature was when I was happiest. As I grew older, I was always comforted in the knowledge that my angels were not too far away. Their energy and spirits both guided and protected me.

It is no wonder, then, that the most exciting photograph I have ever taken would have been while I was walking in a forest. The picture appearing on the front cover of this book was captured on July 15, 2007, while hiking in the Arkansas Ozarks. This was three days before I collapsed with the brain hematoma. I have no doubt that the female figure in the center of the picture is an angel. If you study the photograph closely, you will be able to identify several other human images, not to mention the white light in the top-right corner. *Nothing has been done to alter the picture. This is exactly as it appeared on my camera the day it was taken.*

I have been questioned many times about why it is out of focus. The answer is simple if you think back to our discussion of electromagnetic energy. With the appearance of so many spirits, there was an extreme amount of energy that interfered with the function of my digital camera. Every photo taken before and after is Kodak clear. We will discuss the picture in greater detail later in this chapter. The fact that these spirits appeared to me on that day is yet another validation of spiritual synchronicity and confirmation that there are no coincidences.

The noun *angel* is derived from the Greek word angelos, meaning "messenger," and the biblical interpretation of angels is that they are the messengers of God. I personally cannot imagine our world without angels, but religious teachings show us that there was a time before their existence. It is presumed from scripture that angels were created after the creation of heaven and earth but before the appearance of Adam and Eve. The Bible teaches us in Colossians 1:16, "For in him were all things created in heaven and on earth, visible, and invisible, whether Thrones, or Dominions, or Principalities, or Powers: all things were created by him and in him." Theologians and educators alike acknowledge that these entities are the angels created by God.

Angelology was first developed by the ancient Persians before being adopted by both Christianity and Judaism. A belief in the existence of angels can be found in most religions throughout history.

- Ancient Egyptians constructed their tombs more elegantly than their homes in preparation for the angels who would visit.
- Residents of Sumer, one of the earliest known civilizations, believed the air was filled with spirits and that each Sumerian soul was protected by an angel.

- Taoists believe that angels protect their young and innocent and that good fortune will come to those who pray to their angels. The Taoist guardian spirits act as messengers between the Masters and Rulers of the universe.
- Muslim belief is that God created the angels from His body to serve as light messengers between man and God. The angels act as guardians for each person until death and ask God's forgiveness for those still on earth. These guardian angels also, in the Muslim belief, are the protectors of heaven.

While they may not be called angels by everyone, spirit beings of some form were prominent in ancient mythology and folklore. Whatever the source of religious beliefs, the common theme is that angels are messengers from a higher Being and are around us because of their pure and unconditional love.

Another common thread stretching across time and among religious beliefs is that our creator was a great manager. In order to maintain order and ensure that specialists were assigned where needed, hierarchies were established, and the angels were assigned specific tasks. Depending upon your belief system, there can be anywhere between four to ten or more orders of angels. I have been raised in the belief of nine orders: seraphim, cherubim, thrones, dominions, virtues, powers, principalities, archangels, and angels. These nine orders are further divided into three hierarchies, or choirs.

The first choir is composed of the seraphim, cherubim, and thrones. These angels are of the highest order, and it is believed that they are the heavenly guardians of the God's throne. The seraphim, whose light is so bright that other heavenly beings cannot look at them, are the caretakers of the throne. The cherubim possess a perfect knowledge of God and are the protectors of the light. Scripture describes the cherubim as those standing guard at the entrance to the garden of Eden refusing entrance to Adam and Eve (Gen. 3:24). The thrones serve as symbols of God's justice and authority.

Dominions, virtues, and powers make up the second choir. Dominions are lordships that oversee all nations and only rarely make themselves known to us. They may be distinguished from the other orders because of the orbs of light on their scepters or swords. Dominions are also tasked with regulating the duties of the lower angels. Virtues, represented as the celestial choir, are the supervisors of the universe and oversee the movements of all heavenly bodies. The powers, as their name implies, are warriors against evil. These warrior angels are the bearers of all conscience and the keepers of history. They work with the principalities to ensure an even and balanced distribution of power among mankind.

The third choir is where you find the heavenly messengers and soldier angels: principalities, archangels, and angels. The principalities, in cooperation with the powers, supervise groups of people and are tasked with carrying out orders given to them by the dominions. They also serve as inspiration in the fields of art and science. The archangels are the highest ranking angels and are the guardians of nations and countries. The angels are the lowest order in the hierarchy and the most common form in contact with us earthly mortals. There are many different categories of these angels, and each has its own specific roles and responsibilities as messengers, healers, and protectors. Our personal guardian angels are a part of this choir.

There has been a long-standing debate as to exactly how many archangels exist. While many modern religions differ over the number in existence, they all agree that Archangel Michael is the only angel referred to in the Bible as the archangel. It is also believed that Lucifer was at one time an archangel before his ego caused him to defy God, and he was cast from heaven. It is also speculated, by those who study the Bible, that it was Archangel Michael and his army of angels who actually cast Lucifer and his fallen angels out of heaven and into hell.

Mixed theories and beliefs about how angels physically look have led to a few basic questions.

- Are they larger than life?
- Does the divine white light cause them to glow from within?
- Are they male or female?
- Do they have wings?
- Does everyone have a personal angel?

I believe that the perception of how angels look in a physical form depends upon each person's own belief system. The Bible generally describes them as wingless with only a brief mention of winged entities: "Above it stood the Seraphims: each one had six wings; with twain (two) he covered his face, and with twain he covered his feet, and with twain he did fly" (Isa. 6:2). "Yea, whiles I was speaking in prayer, even the man Gabriel, whom I had seen in the vision at the beginning, being caused to fly swiftly, touched me about the time of the evening oblation" (Dan. 9:21).

Non-Christian religions tend to portray more winged angels in the form of women and children. We are all familiar with the images of Cupid, who shoots his arrows into unsuspecting lovers. It is perhaps because we humans are so visual that we need pictures and symbols in order to help us understand. This may have been the reason for great religious artists, such as Michelangelo and da Vinci, to include wings on angels. It is easier for us mortals to understand them flying if we are able to see wings. Angels are true spirit and, therefore, are not subject to factors such as gravity and other earthly elements. Angels, like other spirits, are able to be anywhere and everywhere at the same time, because there is neither time nor gravity within the universal space. When necessary, angels will appear to each of us in the form that best assists us in understanding the messages they deliver.

Individual perceptions are different. Take, for example, witnesses of an automobile accident. Generally, if three people witnessed the actual crash, there may be three completely different stories about how it happened. The same was true when I began showing the cover picture to people after discovering it on my camera. My girlfriend Mary Lou initially saw what she believed were ghosts. Ministers and mediums who have examined it saw the lady in the center as an angel surrounded by my spirit guide and other past life spirits. I have believed, since that first day, the center image is that of an angel, but I saw her in a complete human form. The other images I lovingly referred to as my *tree people* or *nature spirits*. What I saw as the angel's arms were viewed by medium Lydia Clar as wings. Lydia said that what I interpreted as arms are actually the front of her wings, which are folded behind her. This might very well be the case, because there is nothing resembling hands at the ends of each arm. Aldous Huxley explained it best when he said, "There are things known and there are things unknown, and in between are the doors of perception."

There are many reasons why an angel may make an appearance to us. Carmel Reilly, in her book *True Tales of Angel Encounters*, has included more than one hundred reported angel encounters submitted to her by people from around the world. These remarkable stories offer validation of the work performed by the angelic realm in areas of faith, healing, protection, guidance, and crossing over at the time of death. Reilly states that angels can appear to anyone for any reason. It does not matter what religion is practiced, if at all, and it doesn't matter whether the person believes in angels. This is an excellent and inspiring book composed of real-life human testimonies.

Those describing near-death experiences almost always include seeing a bright, white light and/or the visions of angels or deceased loved ones who have come to assist them in crossing from this life into the next. There is much talk and speculation about an entity referred to as the Angel of Death. I personally do not believe that there is any angelic spirit that chooses when or how we die. We are born into this world bringing with us our own free will, and the decision as to when we exit was determined before we ever took our first breath. Furthermore, the persona associated with an Angel of Death is dark and threatening. Angels are made of divine light and love. Why then would they become demons of darkness that we must fear?

From the moment the spirits appeared on my camera screen, there has only been a feeling of a loving warmth and comfort associated with them. As discussed earlier, angels appear to us in ways best suited to deliver their messages. Although angels are created of the pure white light of divine love, the angel image appearing on the front cover is very clearly wearing a black dress, which is a symbol of death. The message for me, as I now understand it, was that she had come to assist me in crossing over into the light, which appeared in the upper-right corner of the picture. Of course, at the time, I did not think about it in those terms. Why should I? I believed that the universe had already changed. I wasn't planning on going anywhere.

Once I became strong enough following my surgeries, I began to seek paranormal and spiritual experts who might assist me in understanding exactly what my picture represented. Remember that the universe assists us in miraculous ways, and so it was with my search. I was released from the hospital on August 6, and by August 23, the universe had led me to Cathy Geremia, author of *The Spirit of Photography*.

Cathy has always had the ability to see spirits. As a small child, she became afraid of her ability and mentally turned it off. Each time she would see, sense, feel, or hear a spirit, she would become frightened. One year following her father's death, she saw the faces of both her father and her grandmother in a picture that she took of two of her children. It was then that she decided to overcome her fears and began to learn more about the spirit world. As a result, she now teaches the art of spiritual photograph reading, both in person and through online classes. Cathy shared with me that the experience of seeing her father and grandmother caused her to open her eyes, and by studying spirits, she has learned more about the purpose of life itself. The following is an excerpt from her reading of my picture:

The reason for the blur look of the picture is because of the very powerful energy that your angel is bringing through.... She is very beautiful and very large. Angels have an indescribable beauty to them. She is large because she is very close to you and is an important part in your life. She is the angel who is helping you open up your spiritual energy. She places herself in the center of your picture, which shows she is centered in your life. She is guiding you and with you all of the time....

A large tube of energy is coming from the angel's waist, which connects to another spirit. This spirit is the energy of a large male.... He is to the side but behind the angel. Once her work is done with you, which may be soon, this strong male energy is going to continue working with you. The angel represents the gentle, sweet, kind energy of a beautiful, slender woman. The male energy is much more strong and powerful. The angel is blessing the spirit with intuition, teaching, communication, and healing. This is the meaning of the colors. Your very strong spirit guide will take this energy to help you develop your own intuition, teaching, communication, and healing abilities. You may want to look into Reiki or another form of energy healing.

The colors in your picture are very significant. You have a lot of violet and green. The violet represents spirituality and a close connection to heaven, God, Jesus, and Mary. Violet can also show the interest in learning more about the spirit world. The more we learn, the higher we raise our vibrations. The higher our vibration, the closer we are with the spirit world, and the more messages we receive from spirits. The messages could be through pictures, sensing, feeling, dreams, and many more. The green color is healing. You are being blessed from heaven with the violet light, and you are being healed with the green energy light. There is no better way to be healed than with blessings from heaven. The blue light is energy of teaching and communication. You are being blessed to learn more and teach others what you have learned through verbal communication. The pink color is blessings of love. The

> bright white light is more energy from angels and heaven. Bright white light represents the purest energy of love from heaven. You should ask to be surrounded and filled with this white light every day. This is a way of asking for angels to protect us and fill us with love.
>
> *Cathy Geremia, August 23, 2007*

I told Cathy that I was uncertain if the images were visible at the moment that I took the picture or if they had appeared sometime later. She assured me that everything in the picture was there the moment I took it. According to her, once you begin to train yourself to see spirits in pictures and elsewhere, the easier it becomes. Cathy is not a ghost hunter in search of ghostly pictures—they just happen for her during her normal routines. Her amazing pictures have captured deceased family members and pets, nature spirits, spirit guides, angels, and masters. One picture contains three Indian spirits revealing themselves as skeletons. Her orb pictures validate that some orbs are actual spirit energies and not airborne particles of dust or passing insects as we discussed in the last chapter.

As I have already mentioned, I am a high school reading teacher. My students have not only become excited that their teacher is writing a book, but they have truly opened up about paranormal and spiritual experiences that they have had personally. They represent a perfect cross section of genders, cultures, ethnicities, and religions. It is very interesting to listen to their beliefs and attitudes about spiritual visions. I keep a small copy of my angel picture on my desk, and several times each week someone wants to pick it up and talk about it. What I refer to as my angel picture, my students, for the most part, call my ghost picture. Because of statements they have made and questions they have asked, I would now like to shift our direction and discuss the differences between angels and ghosts.

Overview

- The noun *angel* is derived from the Greek word angelos meaning "messenger." The biblical interpretation of angels is that they are the messengers of God.
- Angelology, the study of angels, was first developed by the ancient Persians before being adopted by both Christianity and Judaism.

- Depending upon your belief system, there can be anywhere between four to ten or more orders of angels.
- There are mixed theories and beliefs about how angels physically look.
- Each person's belief system determines how angels look in a physical form. Angels appear to each of us in the form that best assists us in understanding the messages they deliver.
- There are many reasons why an angel may make its appearance. It does not matter what religion is practiced, if at all, and it doesn't matter whether the person believes in angels.
- Those describing near-death experiences almost always include seeing a bright, white light and/or the visions of angels.

<u>Your Psychic Journal:</u>

I would love to be able to read all of your journal entries about angels. Almost everyone I know believes that they have had some type of an encounter with them. What about you? They are all around us to provide guidance and protection.

- Have you or someone close to you had a personal encounter with an angel? Describe the situation.
- Do you believe that your guardian angel has saved you from a harmful or dangerous situation? What was it?
- Have you ever known someone whose life was saved by an angel?

Remember to write whatever comes into your mind, even if you think the incident may have been your imagination.

Think, reflect, and happy journaling!

Chapter Fourteen

Ghosts

Please don't come to my grave and cry.
My body rests here, but I did not die.

I am now free, with each passing season,
To watch and protect you, not needing a reason.
Our friendship survives, and our love will endure.
My loving essence remains; of this you can be sure.

My love may be seen in all flowers that grow.
My smile is as bright as the sparkle of snow.
My voice you can hear in each gentle wind.
My strength you will see in the trees as they bend.

Please don't stand alone and cry.
I am still by your side. I did not die.

It was February 10, 1970, and the clock on the radio indicated that it was 2:31 a.m. I turned my head toward the crib in the corner of the bedroom where my four-week-old daughter was sleeping. My first thought was that I had abandoned my peaceful deep sleep because she was making her wake up and feed me noises. A quick peek in that direction assured me that she was still asleep. I glanced at the pillow next to me and saw my husband snoozing peacefully. Still, I was convinced I had heard something. As my eyes began to focus, I noticed an adult figure standing in the darkened hallway, just outside our bedroom door. Thoughts sprinted through my mind. Who is this in our house in the middle of the night? Am I dreaming? Is it a burglar? Should I scream out for help?

"Who's there?" My eyes were adjusting to the darkness, and I realized that it was my longtime neighborhood friend Joey. "What are you doing here? And … how did you get in?" I questioned in a whispered tone as I pulled the blankets up to cover myself.

Joey had been the boy next door during our high school days. He was also one of those kids who had been blessed with both incredible good looks and a loveable personality. As kids often do, we used to make jokes of his Italian heritage, which had bestowed upon him his black hair, flawless dark olive skin, light blue eyes that always had a twinkle, and a beautiful smile highlighted by his sparkling white teeth. The amount of attention he received because of his physical appearance embarrassed him, making him shy around most people. The last time we had visited with each other, seven or eight months earlier, was just before his Army unit left for active duty in Vietnam.

"Joey? What are you doing here? When did you come home?" I was growing more curious by the second. He would never have just popped in without calling, let alone break into our house in the middle of the night. He was much too polite for that.

"I came to say good-bye. You've always been my special friend, and I love you."

I laid there staring at him as he stood in the darkened doorway. I was hearing his words, but I knew that I was receiving them silently and unspoken. Had he spoken to me in his normal voice, he certainly would have awakened my sleeping husband, and he had not moved. *Okay*, I thought, *he's whispering. After all, it's the middle of the night, and here he is in our house only a few feet outside our bedroom.*

"What?" I whispered again as I sat up gently on the bedside. It was my intention to talk to him in the living room so as not to wake the entire house, although the baby was due to scream for a meal in about an hour. When she was hungry, no one slept!

"I have to go. Remember that I will always be here for you." And then as quickly as he had appeared, he was gone. I walked into the hallway and proceeded to check the other rooms in our small house. No one was there.

The house was completely empty, and the doors were all locked—from the inside.

Okay, Patricia, you are losing it, I thought. I knew this was not a dream, and after all, we *were* just talking to each other. I also knew that I was wide awake and had been looking straight at him. Logic told me that whatever it was that had just taken place was some sort of hallucination. It had to be because there was no way for this to be possible. His military squadron had shipped out months earlier. I slipped back into bed and laid there thinking about this oddly strange event. "Weird." I could not go back to sleep after that and continued talking to myself. "But he was here.... And we did talk to each other. What's happening?"

The remainder of the morning was as normal as can be with a one-month-old and a twenty-two-month-old. I was busying around in the kitchen when I heard the reporter on the midday news say something that truly shook the ground I was standing on.

> Local resident Joseph Michael Bloom, son of Mr. and Mrs. Joseph N. Bloom, was killed overnight in Vietnam. The helicopter in which he was a passenger crashed shortly after take off. Details are sketchy. We are following this story closely and will bring you additional information about this latest war tragedy as we receive it. Stay tuned.

I could not believe what I had just heard. Almost immediately my telephone began ringing with many calls from our other friends. I thought that this was just not possible. I prayed that it was not true, but it was! This was my first encounter communicating directly with the spirit world, although at the time, I had no idea of what was happening. This was a bittersweet time for me. I had just given birth to my second beautiful daughter, and now I had lost one of my best friends to a war that had already taken two of my former classmates. I wondered how I could ever tell anyone that I had both seen and talked to Joey on the same night he was killed thousands of miles away. My mother was the only person I felt comfortable talking to about this incredible event.

For many years, I did not share this story with anyone except Joey's parents and my mother. And even then, I told them only that I had recently had a terrible dream that this was going to happen. I was still living in the shadow of my mother's death visions, and was truly not ready to accept that this *gift* now belonged to me—I was afraid.

That was the only time in my life that I was actually able to see and talk with someone on the other side. I believe that I no longer see spirit in human form because of the intense fear I experienced after seeing Joey. I have now become more of a mental intuitive and do, from time to time, feel the presence of friends and relatives who are no longer in physical form. Although, I now sometimes think that at this stage in my life, it might not be so bad to be able to visit with them again in person.

How much do *you* know about ghosts? When this first began happening to me, I found myself with many more questions than plausible explanations. Many years have passed since Joey's February visit, and his was not my only ghostly encounter. Since then I have had several more spiritual visitors pop in—just not in their physical forms. Ironically, now I seem to be the one that is called upon to provide answers and explanations. The following is a short list of the most frequent questions I am asked.

- What are ghosts?
- How do you talk to them?
- What is the difference between ghosts and demons?
- Are angels, spirits, and ghosts the same?
- Why do ghosts exist?
- Where do they come from?
- Are they good or evil?
- Can they harm us?
- Is there such a thing as a ghostly possession?
- If you see a ghost, does it mean that someone is going to die?

You can probably add even more to this short list, but these represent some of the most common questions.

We have learned in the preceding chapters that the universe is made up of different forms of energy. Humans are unique in that we are both physical and mental energies. Our physical bodies are a composition of different solid elements and energy, which interact with the earth and its gravitational forces. Our spiritual bodies, minds, memories, and souls are pure energy and are not restricted to the confines of the earthly plane. At the time of death, our physical bodies die and remain a part of the earth. Our spiritual bodies immediately move on into another dimensional plane, much like the quantum physics mini vacation from chapter nine.

Most people who have experienced near-death experiences describe what happens when their souls step out of their physical bodies. Whatever their reasons might have been, these people crossed over into the light realm but did not remain. They often describe hovering above their physical bodies watching as doctors fight in an effort to keep them alive, seeing a bright white light, being greeted by angels or family members who have crossed over, or seeing a beautiful green valley filled with people in light-colored, flowing robes. Their physical bodies temporarily died in the physical universe, while their souls momentarily stepped outside the human form and into the spiritual universe. They briefly stepped into heaven and felt its unconditional peace and love. During the minutes while their souls were separated from their bodies, they became ghosts. Psychic James Van Praagh, in his book *Ghosts Among Us*, says that in a sense, we are all ghosts, because we are all spirits residing in physical bodies.[20]

At the moment of death—when the soul leaves the body—it enters the light and becomes spirit. If it does not enter the light, it remains earthbound in the form of a ghost. On certain occasions, however, a spirit that has crossed to the other side may choose to revisit loved ones. There may be times when it is necessary for them to complete unfinished business, to offer guidance or counseling, or to assist loved ones in crossing over when their time has come. We often complain about not having time for closure when dealing with the death of someone close to us, but the deceased also need closure when leaving those whom they deeply cared for. It has taken me many years to fully understand that Joey visited me on that cold February night so that he could say good-bye and leave me with his loving thoughts.

There are a lot of reasons why a soul may become earthbound. A death may have been extremely sudden, such as an accident or murder. In these cases, the ghost may not realize that it is actually dead. There are more ghost stories than can be counted that describe people seeing or feeling the spirit of someone who died tragically. Many of these earthbounds have not left because they do not know they are dead, or they refuse to accept it as a possibility. Others realize they are dead but will not cross into the light because of unfinished business. This might include trying to tell family members where to find the will or where they hid money or other valuables, desiring to be around for an important occasion such as a birth or wedding, and in some cases, where murder was involved, wanting to see their murderer caught and punished.

My husband and I lost a very close family friend a few years ago when he was murdered. He was working nights as a security guard for an internationally acclaimed university. Until he was tragically shot down in

---

20 James Van Praagh, *GHOSTS AMONG US: Uncovering the Truth About the Other Side.* (New York: HarperCollins, 2008), 37.

cold blood during an attempted robbery, there had never been a crime of that magnitude on that campus. In life, he was a true character and larger than life itself. He loved living life to its fullest, and his favorite things included cooking, eating, drinking, and having a good party with his many friends. Following the funeral, his son presented me with a Cajun chef's apron that I had personalized for his father as a Christmas gift a few years before. I now keep it hanging in my kitchen, which is where he liked to hang out. Since his passing, I feel his presence often, especially in the kitchen. On one particular afternoon, I was at home alone and standing at the kitchen counter working on our evening meal. Out of nowhere, I strongly felt his presence. So, being the good-natured friend that I am, I turned around and said, "Hello." I then asked him to give me a sign if he was in fact, present. Almost immediately, across the room from where I was standing, his apron fell from its hanger and was lying in a heap on the floor. Yes, he was there all right!

Because he was so full of life and had no intention of dying at such an early age—especially at the hands of common street punks—I know that he is currently an earthbound spirit. Three young men are known to have been involved in his shooting, and only one of them is currently serving prison time. Knowing our friend as well as I did, I believe that until his soul has been satisfied that justice has been served, he will not cross over. On a lighter note, having his spirit around our house has also convinced me that our personalities survive death. He was a prankster who took great delight in playing jokes on his friends. As with the apron falling to the floor at the moment I asked him to give me a sign, there are many funny little things that continue to happen around our house for no apparent reason. My husband and I usually just laugh, and one of us will say, "He's back!"

Sometimes, when the process of dying is horrific, the soul is unable to move into the light. When this happens, the troubled soul remains earthbound indefinitely. It does not know to move into the light in order to cross to the next plane. Souls such as this are unfortunately given credit for so-called hauntings. The universe, in all its wonder, led me to turn on the Syfy Channel one afternoon, and I was not prepared for what I witnessed. I watched a two-hour documentary titled *Children of the Grave*, which was filmed to uncover the truth behind child ghost hauntings.

The production, created by Philip Adrian Booth and Christopher Saint Booth, was both remarkable and horrific. Their documentary covered a ten-day investigation spanning six states. They visited abandoned orphanages and other sites where graves, identified only by a number, marked the sites where children had been buried. A few of the markers had no identification, and it is speculated that there are possibly hundreds of children buried without even having a plain headstone. Even worse, they may have been buried in mass gravesites. These poor children, left alone without the love of families to care for them, died earthbound and alone with the exception of each other. These lost and tortured little souls desperately need to be led into the light so that they may be freed at last. I, personally, am uncertain as to how much of the photographed evidence was actual, untouched footage, but the message it contained was strong and extremely accurate.

These children could not control their destinies—they were forced upon them. While watching *Children Of The Grave*, I was reminded of the children who perished at the 1886 Crescent Hotel & Spa during the time of Dr. Norman Baker. How many of them, I wondered, are still wandering the halls waiting for someone to lead them into the light? What about Dr. Baker himself and all the other dark souls that led to the deaths of the children and other innocent souls? When an adult has been mean and cruel in life, his soul will remain that way in death. If we are good and loving individuals while alive, that same caring spirit will continue as we move into the light realm.

Are all earthbound ghosts dark and evil? The answer is simple—no, not all of them. We have been raised loving to fear tales of the dark side. Since childhood, Hollywood has bombarded our minds and cultures with films such as *The Exorcist, Rosemary's Baby, The Shining, The Amityville Horror, The House on Haunted Hill*, etc. It is no wonder that so many people live in fear of seeing a ghost or, even worse, being possessed by one. I have heard many cultural beliefs and superstitions about death, dying, and ghosts from my high school students. One, having moved here from the Dominican Republic, told me that you should always make the sign of a cross whenever passing a funeral possession; otherwise, you might be possessed by the dead. Another Dominican belief is that you should always cross yourself for protection and respect at both the beginning and end of a graveyard as you pass by. *This one might very well hold some validity.*

In chapter eight, I talked about the intense emotions that overtook me when I visited my parents' gravesite at the National Cemetery in Little Rock, Arkansas. It was another travel day for me, and I hurriedly packed, unconsciously neglecting to take time for prayer and meditation. This was not wise, and I thought that I knew better. I walked into that cemetery completely open to any negative spirit or ghost desiring to attach itself to me. As quickly as I opened the car door, I was overcome with a powerful mix of extreme sadness and deep, raging anger. This intense rage was not me. I had been possessed even if only for a few very short minutes. Once back in the car, I was able to meditate and ask in prayer to be released of all the negative energies and to be healed in the protective energy of the white light. Almost immediately, I became calm and was back to my normal self once again.

I have numerous students who have moved here from Central American, South American, and Caribbean countries. One Hispanic young man recently asked me, "Mrs. Leffingwell, did you know that I saw a ghost one time?"

"Did you?" I asked curiously.

"Yeah. Me and my cousin saw my great-grandmother's ghost. We were at my auntie's house."

"When was this?"

"About a year ago. Did you know that when you see a ghost, somebody is going to die?" He asked it in such a way that I knew that he was telling me this as fact.

"I have heard of people who see the spirit of a deceased family member just before they die, but I don't believe that everyone who sees a ghost is going to die."

"Yes they are. I have always heard that if you see a ghost, somebody is going to die. My grandmother died right after we saw my great-grandmother."

Children have always been able to see spirits more than adults, because they have not yet been conditioned that what they see is a product of their imaginations. Our American cultural and religious beliefs have unfortunately stolen these gifts from our children. My international students move here from totally different cultural systems and bring with them completely different understandings of the spiritual and paranormal. In fact, most of those students seem to have a much better understanding and respect for the spirit world than do many of our homegrown kids. However, this conversation started me thinking about how a ghost might be able to negatively affect our health and well-being.

I am a lightworker and therefore choose to only deal with spirits of the light. I am very much aware that there is good and evil in everything, and so it is also with earthbound ghosts. My dark, emotionally charged experience in the cemetery is a perfect example. I have stressed numerous times that our spiritual being is all energy. This inner energy, oftentimes referred to as Chi, is found spinning in different areas of our physical bodies. These energy centers are the chakras. Whenever someone says that you have a bright aura, they are referring to the colors associated with the electromagnetic vibrational field surrounding your physical body created by the chakra centers. Your aura changes colors and levels of brightness mirroring any changes within the chakras. By learning more about the function of the individual chakras, you will be able to understand how they may affect your personality and health. You will also become able to detect what is really your energy and what might be the energy of someone else, such as the psychic vampires mentioned earlier. There are many excellent books and CDs on the market that both explain the function of each chakra and offer techniques to keep them clean and balanced.

There are literally hundreds of energy chakras in our spiritual bodies, with seven main, primary centers. Chakras are a series of spinning energy wheels, each representing a different color. They are lined up parallel to but behind the spinal column of the physical body. Together they represent the seven primary colors of the rainbow. It is important to keep the chakras in line and well-balanced if you want to remain mentally and physically healthy. An out of balance chakra system may be the catalyst for coming down with a sudden illness, feeling the blues or depression for no apparent reason, or experiencing fear, guilt, paranoia, etc. Dark energy earthbound ghosts seek out those with weak chakras, Chi, and attach themselves just because they can.

To describe each of the chakras in detail would best be left to another book dedicated solely to that topic. In order to help your understanding, we will take a closer examination as to what happened to me in the cemetery when I left my chakras completely unprotected. I have no idea who the ghost was that attached itself to me, but, based on the dates of the grave markers, I would say that it died between the years of 1890 and 1920. Remembering that our personalities remain with our souls when we die, I would guess that in life this ghost was a very angry person whose only way of control was through fear. He has now had more than one hundred years to continue blaming everyone else for anything that happened to him. Ghosts get their strength from our energies, especially when there are no other sources available. How thrilled he must have been when I showed up, completely unprotected and unsuspecting.

Because of the extreme emotions of sadness and intense anger I felt, I am certain that the ghost attached itself to my heart chakra. The heart chakra is the fourth chakra and is, as its name implies, located in the center of the chest. It is associated with the color green, which represents healing and love. Its function is to connect the higher spiritual chakras with the lower physical and mental centers. When clean and in balance, this chakra emits a feeling of being one with life, a true sense of identity, and complete openness and unconditional love. This is the ideal state when this chakra is working properly.

When the dark energy of this hundred-year-old ghost attached its ugly, dark energy to my heart chakra, the exact opposite happened. I have never felt so sad and angry in my entire life. Had I not already studied chakra balancing and meditation techniques, I probably would not have returned from the slump so quickly. What is worse, I might very well have continued carrying that negative energy around with me until I dumped it on some other poor soul, while I remained totally unaware that anything had happened. I would then have become a psychic vampire. More than likely, I would have rationalized that I became so emotional because I was visiting the graves of my mom and dad. The emotion that took over me was not a normal, healthy emotion. What I experienced was from extreme darkness and was worse than anything I can even relate, because it is beyond my frame of reference. It was bad.

The point to be made here is that there are nice ghosts who have been touched by the light, and there are dark, not so nice ghosts who prefer to continue controlling people through fear tactics, just as they did while alive. A person who is good in life will not become a dark earthbound ghost in death. It just does not work that way. However, a person who might have committed a few injustices while living, may hang around for a while as an earthbound ghost until they make the wrongs they committed right again. Once those tasks are completed, they will also cross over into the light.

The moral to this chapter is to not fear ghosts, whether they are good or naughty. The good are only here to watch or help us. The dark earthbounds cannot hurt or harm us as long as we take proper measures to protect ourselves with prayer, meditation, and a blanket of white light. The universe is a very big place, and there is plenty of room for all of us, visible and invisible, to live peacefully.

Overview

- Our spiritual bodies, minds, memories, and souls are pure energy. Our physical bodies are made up of solid elements.
- When the physical body dies, it remains a part of the earth. The spiritual body (soul) immediately moves on into another dimensional plane. If the soul does not move to the spiritual realm, it remains earthbound and becomes a ghost.
- A deceased person does not become an angel.
- A near-death experience occurs when the soul momentarily leaves the physical body and then returns.
- A spirit that has crossed to the other side may choose to revisit loved ones to offer guidance and counseling or to assist loved ones in crossing over when their time has come.
- In some cases, when the death was tragic, the soul may need to return to say last good-byes to loved ones or complete unfinished business.
- If the process of dying was horrific, the soul may be unable to move into the light and will remain earthbound indefinitely. It may not know that it has died.
- The personality is pure energy and will continue on after death. Hauntings or possessions may be the result of an earthbound spirit who was also mean and hurtful in the physical realm. Likewise, a jovial personality will live that way in the spirit realm.
- Meditation, prayer, and surrounding yourself with divine light are ways of protecting yourself from possessions of negative energies and spirits.
- *Do not* be fearful of ghosts. *Do* learn how to recognize when they are present. Some of them may simply want your help in crossing over to the other side.

Your Psychic Journal:

Here we are again—time for you to write in your psychic journal. One thing is certain. If you have ever encountered a ghost, you will not have to think too hard to remember it. Even though ghosts are all around us, its not that often that we are able to see them, hear them, or communicate with them.

- What is your ghost story?
- Did this happen to you or to someone you know?
- Where did your encounter happen?
- Was the ghost visible, or did you know it was present due to its energies?
- Did you know the ghost, or was it a complete stranger?
- Did you have any physical effects caused by its presence?
- Have others had similar experiences at the same location?
- Was there a special message that you believe the ghost wanted you to know?

Try to include as many details as you can remember. Include dates, times, locations, weather conditions, people with you, and any other details that you can remember.

Think, reflect, and happy journaling!

Chapter Fifteen

Synchronicity and Symbols

"... in each of our lives occur mysterious coincidences ... sudden, synchronistic events that, once interpreted, lead us into our true destiny."
James Redfield, The Celestine Prophecy

When the universe first guided me to write this chapter on synchronicity, I knew that it was to be an important part of this entire story. However, I sat for several days staring at my blank computer screen, praying, meditating, and thinking about ways to present it. My ah-ha moment came while having a discussion with my close friend Thom about the different paths we have each taken in our lives and how those experiences led us to become who we now are. *Thom first began to see spirits when he was seventeen, following the death of his grandfather.* It then became crystal clear that this chapter was not to begin with explanations for why I began studying the spiritual and paranormal. It was not to be about how I ended up sitting in Reverend Zanghi's office hearing the message, "You were scheduled to die, but the universe has changed." It was also not about how or why Mary Lou and I decided to make our trip to Eureka Springs, Arkansas, where I was to photograph my angel and spirit guides. And it wasn't about collapsing in New Orleans from a massive brain bleed. My story of spiritual synchronicity, in this lifetime, began at my birth. I then understood that I must begin at the beginning.

My mother and father were not physically large. At the time she passed, mother was only four feet ten inches, and my father was little more than five feet four or five inches tall. I, on the other hand, took all of my genetic inheritance from the much taller side of the family tree. Although I am unaware of the many difficulties Mom had while pregnant with me, I have been told that she was in full labor for two complete days, and that I was not cooperating. Physically, I was much too large for her to deliver normally, and to make matters worse, I was in a breech position. Those two facts alone made it an extremely difficult birth.

While the doctors and nurses were trying everything possible to turn me around, I was determined to enter the world feet first and face up. This type of delivery, in those days, was difficult for a normal-sized woman, and because my mother was so small, there was not much room for maneuvering me around. Caesarean births were not commonplace at that time and were also extremely dangerous. At some point, I became wedged in the birth canal, and my mother began to hemorrhage. The delivering doctor at last felt he had to meet with my father in the waiting room. He was very concerned about what was happening and wanted my father to make a decision. Either they would be able to save my mother, or they would be able to save me, but there seemed to be very little possibility that both of us would survive.

My father, as the story goes, became enraged and ordered the doctor to save both of us. He would not hear of either one of us dying. He told the doctor to do whatever he had to do to make that happen. There were no other options. Following a few more trying hours in delivery, I was born at 10:03 p.m., weighing in at eight pounds and measuring twenty inches long. Mom had to spend some additional time in the hospital recovering from her ordeal, but my father got his wish. We all went home from the hospital healthy and happy.

Mom, much to her chagrin, was not able to have other children after having undergone such a physically traumatic childbirth. But, to her credit, she became determined that I would not grow up being a spoiled only child. She believed in the cliché, spare the rod and spoil the child. She kept me on a short leash during all of my childhood years, and for that, I am extremely grateful. My personal message that I have carried forward from entering this world in the way I did is that I must always stand on my own two feet and face whatever comes at me with courage. I was to learn that nothing would ever come easy for me, and there were to be no shortcuts.

Had my father agreed with the doctor that either mother or child could have been saved, I would not be sitting here telling you this story. Synchronicity was at work, and therefore, my father made the decision that we would both live. There are no coincidences, and everything happens for a reason. I am here because of the love between my mother and father, and I am here today because God has a divine purpose for me to still be here.

The universe speaks to us in many ways. Sometimes, it is God's way of answering our prayers, and in other ways, it is providing us with guidance or protection. Once the messages have been sent, it then becomes our responsibilities to receive them and understand their meanings. The messages may come to us as thoughts, soft whispers, or dreams, and they may arrive in other, more physical ways such as chance encounters with people, places, events, or animals. Synchronicity is the way the soul guides us and gives confirmation that we are on the right path.

What exactly is synchronicity? The term was coined by Carl Jung, a Swiss-born psychiatrist and psychologist. He described it as being a series of separate and unsimilar events that occur simultaneously but, when examined closely, are found to have a meaningful relationship to each other. These events cannot be linked to a cause and effect theory but are blended together in a simultaneous, unexplainable, but meaningful way. Jung's theory of synchronicity states that a person is intuitively able to make a connection between objective manifestations in the physical world and the subjective ones in the spiritual world. He believes that there is a dimension beyond time where our spirits and minds merge with matter. These meaningful coincidences, according to Jung, are only the surface of a much deeper reality.

Synchronistic messages can supply us with information to make immediate decisions, or they can, over a period of time, help us to have a much greater vision and understanding of life. I have reached the age now where I can reflect on situations that I have encountered and on the various people who have come and gone in my life. When viewing these experiences from my current vantage point, it becomes easy to see the synchronistic effects.

For example, as a small child, I was raised in the Baptist church. As I became an adolescent, I moved my membership to a nearby Methodist congregation, which came as a great surprise to my parents, who had no idea this had taken place until they were visited by members of my new church. Then, in my earlier adult years, Catholicism called me to change religions and raise my children in this faith. Over the course of my early childhood and teenage years, my parents allowed me to visit church services with my friends. I was able to experience Lutheran, Episcopal, Latter Day Saints, Mormon, Pentecostal, Catholic, and other faiths. In high school, as part of a debate class, we randomly drew a topic to research in preparation for our great debate at the end of the term. Synchronicity was at work again, and I drew world religions. For the next eight weeks, I had to research religions such as Buddhism, Hinduism, Islam, Greek Orthodox, etc.

Is it a coincidence that I am now able to benefit from this basic foundation and understanding of so many beliefs and faiths? I do not think it is coincidence. The spiritual universe is filled with energy frequencies of all faiths, and now, thanks to its synchronistic distribution of knowledge over time, I have a greater appreciation for each and every one of them.

Synchronicity oftentimes manifests its actions in short bursts of meaningful coincidences. One evening while I was working on the "soul searching" chapter, it became obvious to me that I needed additional information about Albert Einstein and his theories of relativity. I made a mental note to go to the local bookstore after school the following day. The next morning, I needed to make copies of a test during my planning period and walked across campus to the faculty workroom. As my luck would have it, both of the copy machines were out of order. I needed to have the tests by the following morning, so I decided to trek back across campus to the library in hope of using that copy machine.

As it happened, the librarian had been inventorying books and was preparing to send old materials to the book depository. She placed a few of the better ones on a cart near the front door with a sign reading "Free Books." Because, and only because I was coming from the workroom, it was necessary for me to use the front door entrance on the north side of the building, although I usually enter from the east entrance, which is near my classroom. I walked past the book cart on my way to the copy room and happened to notice a book buried in the back of the cart: *Albert Einstein In His Own Words*. Synchronicity? Definitely. Through a series of completely unrelated events, I received a resource even better than what I was going to be shopping for later in the day. This book was a compilation of two complete books, *Relativity* and *Out of My Later Years*. The librarian had no idea that I was looking for this information, and I would not have walked past that cart had the copy machines in the faculty lounge been functional. This is a perfect example of two separate and unlike events occurring simultaneously in different locations that together had a meaningful relationship to each other, which only I could understand. I call that synchronicity.

Oftentimes, synchronicity involves elements other than humans in delivering messages. Robert Aziz describes in his book, *C. G. Jung's Psychology of Religion and Synchronicity*, how a wife of one of Jung's patients mysteriously witnessed a flock of birds gather at the death room windows when both her mother and grandmother passed. This was, by all outward appearances, considered a coincidence, but it was a story that Jung had previously heard from others. His patient was developing new symptoms, which, individually, were minor but, together, might have indicated a possible heart problem. Jung sent the patient to a specialist who examined him and declared him to be in good health. The patient was walking back to Dr. Jung's office with a note from the specialist in his pocket, when he collapsed from a heart attack. As Jung told the story, the wife was in an anxious state of mind even before they brought her dying husband home. Earlier that afternoon, after her husband left for the doctor's office, a flock of birds landed on their house. Was she reacting because of a strong belief in superstition, or was the arrival of the birds truly a message to her that death was imminent?

Throughout time, symbols have been used as the universal language. No matter what country one may travel to, whether or not he speaks the language, symbols remain the same. Airlines use the symbol of seatbelts to tell us either that we should remain buckled up or that it is safe to unbuckle and move around the cabin. Recently, in the United States, no smoking symbols have been posted almost everywhere we go. There are symbols we recognize immediately that tell us to recycle, handicapped parking, hospital zone, children crossing, no parking, no U-turns, stop, playground area, picnic area, etc. Most of these symbols have been so ingrained in us, that both our conscious and our unconscious minds recognize them and understand their meanings.

Synchronicity is the universe's way of using nature as symbols in its effort to communicate. I have learned that everything in nature speaks to us, oftentimes providing insights into our own lives. Animals, reptiles, and insects each have their own individual meanings to us. The remainder of this chapter reviews the synchronicity of nature's messages to me during those final five days leading up to my collapse and concludes with a valuable lesson taught to me by the dragonfly immediately upon my return home from the hospital.

Butterfly

The first day of our Ozark Mountain pilgrimage found Mary Lou and I exploring beautiful Branson, Missouri, and surrounded by a multitude of butterflies in all sizes, shapes, and colors. Everywhere we went, we were surrounded by these fairylike creatures. It was difficult to watch them flittering about from one flower to the next without feeling a sense of happiness.

The symbolism of the butterfly represents change, joy, and color. It has, throughout history, been associated with spiritual transformation. Its short life span sends the message that we should strive to be happy, and to live life to the fullest. The butterfly also teaches us that we should always be prepared to make changes, especially in times of crisis.

Today, many cultures share religious or superstitious beliefs surrounding the magical powers of the butterfly. Recently, an international news reporter recounted the story of two Chilean miners who reported seeing a white butterfly only moments before the walls of their thirteen foot wide tunnel collapsed around them. As the dust settled, the men maneuvered their truck around the fallen rock and finally joined the other thirty-one miners who were safely gathered together in their underground shelter. They believed that if they had not stopped their truck, at the precise moment when they saw the butterfly, they would have certainly been killed. No one was able to offer an explanation as to how this small, white butterfly had flown more than 1,640 feet deep into the mine. *Was this a divine messenger sent to warn them of impending danger?*

For me, the Branson butterflies were telling me that I needed to relax, and, like them, enjoy the joyous dance of life by experiencing new opportunities whenever they arise. By the end of our first day, I was already feeling the butterfly medicine's soothing effects as it began healing my soul.

Mountains

I love the mountains and always have. After all, I was born in the Ozarks. I am always awestruck by their beauty and strength. *This coming from someone who now lives where the highest roadway is a bridge crossing the Indian River at sea level.* My friend and I drove along winding back-roads as we traveled south from Branson to our final destination of Eureka Springs. At one location, I asked Mary Lou to pull over and stop so that we could spend a few minutes being up close and personal with the grandeur created by Mother Nature.

A mountain may be symbolic of a problem or challenge in our life. When we see the mountain as large, inflexible and unmoving, we develop fears of failure, causing us to runaway or hide from the problem. We may also worry about the unknowns waiting for us on the other side of the mountain. However, the mountain also teaches us courage, commitment, and patience. Once we climb to the top, the panoramic view provides us with a greater perspective on life and its challenges. When we are able to see life as the big picture, we quickly learn not to be so serious about the mundane, daily details.

Mountains represent our connection between heaven and earth and teach us that if we can overcome all of our earthly challenges, we will be certain of receiving spiritual enlightenment and blessings from heaven.[21] It has always been the desire of people to build at the highest peaks in order to enjoy the views and to feel closer to God.

Clouds

As we drove, we passed through several layers of clouds. We stopped and got out of the car at a roadside observation site, and, as we walked, we could feel the cool mist caressing our skin.

Clouds are a mixture of the four basic elements—fire, earth, air, and water. Our moods are affected by clouds based on their composition of these four elements. Light, fluffy, little, white clouds make you feel happy and full of energy. Dark, oppressive, threatening storm clouds create a cause for alarm. Clouds are ever changing. They form and then disappear without a trace. From this, we learn transformation and forgiveness. For those of us who struggle with a troubling memory or severe guilt, we should become more like the clouds. Let the past become the past, and do not let it "cloud" the present. Life presents us with our own personal dark clouds from time to time, and when that happens, we need to remember that they are only a temporary. Our happy, little, puffy, white clouds will quickly return.

Cloud mist is a symbol of our ever-changing spiritual growth, separating the visible and invisible worlds. A message to us from the clouds is that we must remove our own clouds of ignorance in order for true enlightenment to shine through. *I was unaware of it on this particular day, but I was about to take several walks between the clouds during the next two days.*

21 Andrews, 62–63.

Eagle

As we stood in the mist of a cleansing cloud, we watched as a bald eagle soared first above us and then out over the valley before vanishing into a cloud below it.

The eagle is a symbol of freedom and spirituality. Native Americans have long considered the eagle and its feathers to be sacred. The eagle teaches a connection between earth and sky. If you have an eagle totem, or one enters your life suddenly, you should strive for balance in all aspects of your life. Eagle medicine prepares us to become more creative, passionate, and spiritual. Many healers have the eagle as their animal totem. When a soaring eagle enters your life, it is preparing you for a spiritual test. This test will challenge your fears and weaknesses, but when you have passed the universe's test, your soul will also soar at a spiritually higher level.

Eagles have always represented power and divine spirit, and as with angels, eagles are considered to be messengers from heaven. As I stood there in complete silence watching the beautiful bird, I was receiving my eagle lesson: In life, we must experience both the highs and lows before we are able to fully understand our true life purpose. *This was July 14 and definitely one of the highs...four days later I would find myself balancing with a tremendous low.*

Deer

As we continued our back-road journey, we saw an unusual quantity of deer. Some stood on the side of the road watching us, while others ran across the road as we approached. I was reminded of a Native American legend that teaches that deer will "lure its hunters deep into the wilderness until they become lost and find themselves embarking on a new adventure."[22]

Deer, by their nature, represent a sense of gentleness which teaches observation, trust, and compassion. When a deer enters your life, you may be receiving confirmation of your own trusting and compassionate soul. Likewise, the message may be that you need to devote more time strengthening your unconditional love for all living things, in order to become more trusting and compassionate.

Deer antlers drop once each year. Antlers are symbols of a higher spiritual connection and convey a message that closer "attention should be given to thoughts and perceptions"[23] that will manifest. Faith should be placed in the truth and accuracy of these new manifestations.

22 Andrews, 262.

23 Andrews, 263.

Deer are known for having extreme senses of vision and hearing. If you have a deer totem you are more than likely highly intuitive. Clairvoyants often speak of their deer power animals that assist them in the spirit world. *I remembered the deer I encountered on the Magnolia Trail and how it stood looking at me as though it knew me. I then completely understood the deep, trusting compassion of deer medicine.*

Cat

From the time we arrived at the 1886 Crescent Hotel & Spa, we were greeted and entertained by the hotel's feline population. I am a cat owner, and I fully understand their mysterious natures and total independence.

Due to the composition of their eyes, they have superb light perception that allows them to see in the dark. Because light is a form of energy, it is believed that cats are also able to see other energies that the human eye cannot. These energies may be human auras, spirit guides, spirits of lost loved ones, ghosts, or orbs. This is a primary reason why cats have been so closely associated with the paranormal. I have watched my own cat chase something through the house that only he can see. At other times, he will sit and stare at something just above the top of my head, leaving me to wonder who or what is up there.

It is believed that cats have energy fields which move in the opposite direction of human energies. This reverse motion is said to have healing effects since it can neutralize energies harmful to people. Several scientific studies have confirmed that cat owners suffering from certain illnesses or injuries heal in less time than non-cat owners. According to the studies, the cat's purring serves as a vibrational therapy system which aids in the faster healing.

If a small, furry, feline enters your life, be prepared for mystical and magical experiences. Cats bring with them an increased sense of curiosity, adventure, and confidence.

Roadrunner

On our first morning in Eureka Springs, I went for an early morning hike and was joined by a very friendly roadrunner. He had been named Rudy by the locals.

The roadrunner is a southwestern species, and it is rare for them to exist in this region. "It is a member of the cuckoo family, and has strong feet and legs allowing it to run with speeds up to eighteen miles per hour. This ground speed and agility is why the Roadrunner is one of few animals that have rattlesnakes as its prey. The Roadrunner's message is to always be alert and thinking on your feet. When this bird enters your life, there will be an increase in energy which will facilitate thought manifestations. It then becomes important to use Roadrunner medicine by being able to stop what you are doing, assess the situation, shift directions, and then run at top speed if the situation becomes threatening."[24] *My strong-footed, quick-thinking, mentally agile, feathered friend joined me only thirty minutes before my angel and spirit picture manifested on the screen of my little Kodak.*

Seagulls

Watching the seagulls from my hospital room window was healing therapy. They seemed to show up every day to entertain me, and their comical antics certainly kept me from becoming depressed. They were also highly visible on the day that Ralph brought me home to begin my recuperation. Once, I actually had the thought that they appeared to be traveling along with our car, almost as though they were our escort home.

Seagulls were known, by the early Celtics, to be messengers from the gods. These messengers linked the world of living to the world of spirit. Spiritually, the beach is considered to be a mystical location between land and sea. It is an intermediary realm, which is the home of many nature spirits, and it is the role of the seagulls to become our communicators within this intermediate realm.

The seagull is a water bird, and water is symbolic of our emotional health. Whenever a gull comes into your life, you should examine any emotional issues surrounding you—past, present, or future. Possibly you need to let go of some old emotional baggage, or it may mean that something is about to happen in your life which will require your increased emotional strength. Seagulls also teach that fairness and respect are key elements for maintaining a strong emotional health. Seagulls produce sounds resembling loud, happy laughter. If a seagull enters your life, learn to "go with the flow." Lighten up, and by all means, do not be too serious. Enjoy life.

Pelican

At one point, as Ralph was driving me home from the hospital, we observed beautiful, brown pelicans cruising gracefully along the edge of the river, and then, without warning, they would dive headfirst into the

24 Andrews, 189.

water, ending in what appeared to be a crash. Soon, they resurfaced with a fish securely trapped in the net of their bills.

Physically, the large pelican does not look like it should float; however, it is extremely buoyant. The message of pelican medicine tells us that no matter how difficult life can become, we will not sink. We will rise above all problems and not drown in a sea of pity. The person with a pelican totem will always rise to the surface, be unselfish, and promote teamwork in all aspects of life.

If a pelican mysteriously appears in your life, you should become aware of any emotional turmoil. This emotional weight has a negative effect on your ability to stay afloat. You would do well to heed the lessons of the seagull in order to rid yourself of emotional issues.

Blue Heron

Having just returned home from the hospital, I walked outside onto our deck to enjoy some much needed, healing, fresh air and sunshine. Fishing, just off of our bulkhead, was a beautiful Blue Heron. It was wading with its feet invisible under the water and was supported only by its long, thin legs. *I was reminded of the message I received at the time of my birth which told me that I too would always have to stand on my own two feet. In many ways, my recent surgeries were symbols of a spiritual rebirth—the ending of one era and the beginning of a new life.*

The heron's blue color combined with its long, curved neck, reflect the fifth chakra. The throat chakra is the center for communication and is the link between our spiritual and creative beings. The color blue is associated with a sense of health, creativity, and self-expression. Blue Heron medicine brings about an increased feeling of calmness, which assists in seeking truthful information and allowing for creative ways to communicate this knowledge.

If you have a Blue Heron as your spiritual totem, you often seek out and plan for moments of quiet and solitude, in order to enjoy inner peace and tranquility. Your solitary uniqueness may, at times, seemingly alienate you from friends and family. At other times, your aloofness tends to disappear when you exhibit strong, self-confident, effective, leadership qualities. Your ongoing challenge is finding balance between having quality time alone with yourself, and time for healthy social interaction with others.

Dragonfly

As I was pointing at the Blue Heron, and in that flash of a moment, (and as if on cue), a huge, bright blue dragonfly flew in and landed on my pointing index finger. I stood there amazed, looking at this gorgeous creature of God as it rested from flight.

"Dragonfly medicine requires that we spend time outside in the sun near fresh water in order to restore and improve health conditions. It calls on us to change our lives, and embrace our deeper feelings so that we will have a greater compassion for ourselves and others. Due to the developmental cycle of the dragonfly, remaining in the larvae stage for two complete years before transforming into a colorful adult, the dragonfly delivers a similar timely message. It says that the person for whom it has become a totem may be entering a two year stage of developing and completing an important creative project."[25] *As I sit writing this final chapter, it has now been twenty-three months since that beautiful blue dragonfly landed on my finger. This is one more validation of nature's intrinsic way of using synchronicity to deliver its messages.*

If you have dragonfly in your life, you should consider taking classes to further develop your psychic or clairvoyant abilities. Take things slowly and do not rush the learning process. You would be wise to spend time in daily meditation. Like the butterfly, the dragonfly life span is short. The message then is to enjoy life to its fullest, wear lots of color, and spread joy wherever you go. Positive thoughts breed positive outcomes.

History has shown us that our ancestors had a close and wonderful connection with nature. Science and technology has, over time, removed us from these natural roots. It has become too easy for us to sit in front of a computer screen for hours, surf television channels without even walking across the room, pick up our cell phones instead of making personal visits to friends or family members, and take for granted all of God's natural gifts. Messages are being sent to us each day—important messages that will go unnoticed unless we take the time to realign ourselves with our natural environment. The universe only speaks to us in ways that we are able to understand. We need only to watch and listen for what is being said. Before science took the spirituality and mysticism away from nature, humans were very connected to Mother Earth. Many of today's world cultures, including Native Americans,

25 Andrews, 340–42.

believe and celebrate a oneness with nature. We should all learn from these cultures, for within their beliefs, we will find the true keys to understanding.

Overview

- Synchronicity is a series of separate and unsimilar events that occur simultaneously but are found to have a meaningful relationship to each other.
- Synchronicity is the way the soul guides us and gives confirmation that we are on the right path.
- Synchronistic messages can supply us with information to make immediate decisions or help us to have a much greater vision and understanding of life.
- Symbols are used as the universal language. Nature symbols are oftentimes the universe's way to communicate.
- The universe only speaks to us in ways that we are able to understand. We need only to watch and listen for what is being said.
- Many of today's world cultures, including Native Americans, believe and celebrate a oneness with nature. We should all learn from these cultures, for within their beliefs, we will find the true keys to understanding.
- There are no coincidences.

Keeping Your Psychic Journal:

Synchronicity is proof that there are no coincidences. Everything happens for a reason, and people come and go in our lives for a special purpose. What synchronistic events did you remember while reading this chapter? Write them down. You will discover that the more you write, the more the memories will surface.

What about symbols? I am not talking about superstitions, such as four-leaf clovers or black cats at Halloween. I am talking about symbols such as the dragonfly, owls, hawks, snakes, roadrunners, etc.—those symbols that Native Americans refer to as totems. Animals, in spirit, guide and watch over us, protecting us while we are living in this earthly plane. Do you collect figurines or pictures of any specific type of animal only because you like them? These animals may be your animal totems. You are attracted to them for a specific reason. Have fun thinking about your entries before you begin writing. Remember, nothing is a coincidence.

Think, reflect, and happy journaling!

Reflections

By three methods we may learn wisdom:
First, by reflection, which is noblest;
Second, by imitation, which is easiest;
and Third, by experience, which is the bitterest.
Confucius

What is life?
It is the flash of a firefly in the night.
It is the breath of a buffalo in the wintertime.
It is the little shadow which runs across
the grass and loses itself in the sunset.
Crowfoot, Blackfoot warrior and orator

It has now been a little more than three years since my surgeries, and physically, I have fully recovered. My hair has grown back and, quite surprisingly, now covers the long crescent scar dividing the left and right sides of my head. Most people, unless they have known me for a while, would never suspect what I underwent. I have been asked many times if I had a near-death experience. Did I see the light? Did I have an out-of-body experience? To those questions, my answer is always the same. "No." My experience was quite the opposite. While everyone close to me, friends and family, worried that I might not survive, I never for one minute considered that as a possibility. Although I knew that I may have been scheduled to die, I also knew that the universe had changed.

Spiritually, I have grown much stronger. The night following my second surgery—when I was awakened by the woman with the warm hands and told that I was a miracle—I knew that I had been touched by an angel and that my work on earth was only beginning. I now know, without a doubt, that there are spirits and angels around us each and every day. I have seen them in the form of orbs and as animal spirits in the forest. They have appeared to me in human form in photographs and as voices that come to me as thoughts. Whenever I see flashes of white or blue lights, I know that angels are near. They are here to protect us and are ready, willing, and able to help us whenever we need them. All we need to do is ask.

I have learned to listen to my spirit guides, which help me avoid problems before they actually happen. In the past, I often ignored numerous spiritual messages, which would have prevented most—if not all—of the negative things that I have ever experienced had I only listened to them. Instead, it appeared easier to ignore the messages, allow negative things to happen to me, and then accept them as facts of life. Looking at it from this perspective makes no sense whatsoever, but that is truthfully how it was. Unfortunately, I still see many people who are continuing to do the same thing, totally unaware how much easier life would be if they began to listen.

The writing of this book has been both a labor of love and an illuminating experience. When I first began, I thought that I would be writing a book about ghosts and other psychic phenomenon in the traditional literary sense. What has evolved is a story of angels, healing powers, meditation, and spiritual growth. I have learned a lot about myself and life through this process. In the beginning, I did not believe that I had true psychic gifts, but I now know otherwise. I feel blessed to have been given the opportunity to review my life through this writing instead of after I have passed. Perhaps that is what Reverend Zanghi meant when he told me that I would be able to understand in life what most people do not see until after they have crossed over. I also know that the writing of this book is one of the reasons that I was given a second chance. God speaks to each of us through the universe in a myriad of ways each and every day. We must be willing to listen and understand when it does.

Resources

Arkansas:

1886 Crescent Hotel & Spa
75 Prospect Avenue
Eureka Springs, Arkansas 72632
Telephone: 800-342-9766
http://www.crescenthotel.com

America's Most Haunted Hotel
1886 Crescent Hotel & Spa
75 Prospect Avenue
Eureka Springs, Arkansas 72632
Telephone: 800-342-9766
http://www.americasmosthauntedhotel.com

The Eureka Springs Ghost Tours
P.O. Box 189
Eureka Springs, Arkansas 72632
Telephone: 479-253-6800
http://www.eureka-springs-ghost.com

Florida:

Brian Curl
BLC Photography
Palm Bay, Florida 32905
Email: bc858curl@cfl.rr.com
http://www.blcphotography.com/BLC_Photography/HOME.html

Cassadaga Spiritualist Camp
Cassadaga, Florida
http://www.cassadaga.org

Lydia Clar, World-renowned Psychic and Author
P.O. Box 410636
Melbourne, Florida 32941-0636
Telephone: 321-253-6156
http://www.lydiaclar.com

Matthew Medium, Psychic and Spiritualist
Matthew Greene
119 Temple Street
Deland, Florida 32720
Telephone: 386-734-4580
http://www.matthewmedium.com

Recommended Books:

Animal Speak
The Spiritual & Magical Powers of Creatures Great & Small
Ted Andrews
Llewellyn, 2007

Beyond Photography
Encounters with Orbs, Angels, and Mysterious Light-Forms!
Katie Hall and John Pickering
O Books, 2006

Black Elk Speaks
Being the Life Story of a Holy Man of the Oglala Sioux
John G. Neihardt (Flaming Rainbow)
University of Nebraska Press, 1972

Coming Out Of Your Psychic Closet
How To Unlock Your Naturally Intuitive Self
Lynn B. Robinson, PhD
Factor Press, 1994

Ghosts Among Us
Uncovering The Truth About The Other Side
James Van Praagh
Harper One, 2008

How to Photograph the Paranormal
Leonore Sweet, PhD
Hampton Roads, 2005

Many Lives, Many Masters
The True Story of a Prominent Psychiatrist, His Young Patient, and the Past-Life Therapy that Changed Both Their Lives
Brian L. Weiss, MD
Fireside, 1988

Out of Darkness, Into Light
My Personal Journey into the Realm of Spirit
Lydia Clar
iUniverse, 2009

The Seat of the Soul
Gary Zukav
Fireside, 1990

The Spiritual Universe
One Physicist's Vision of Spirit, Soul, Matter, and Self
Fred Alan Wolf, PhD
Moment Point, 1999

Bibliography

AllWords.com. Definition: Universe. Dictionary content provided from Wiktionary.org under the GNU Free Documentation License. Allwords © 1998–2009. http://www.allwords.com.

Andrews, Ted. *Animal Speak: The Spiritual & Magical Powers of Creatures Great & Small: © 2007.* Llewellyn Worldwide, Ltd. 2143 Wooddale Drive, Woodbury, MN 55125-2989. All rights reserved, used by permission of the publisher.

Augustine, Saint, Bishop of Hippo. *Confessions of Saint Augustine.* Translated by Rex Warner. New Kensington: Whitaker House, 1996.

Aziz, Robert. *C. G. Jung's Psychology of Religion and Synchronicity.* Albany: SUNY Press, 1990.

Bell, Alexander Graham. *Alexander Graham Bell and the Octet Truss.* Web site maintained by Synergetics on the Web, http://www.grunch.net/synergetics/bell.html.

Booth, Christopher Saint, and Philip Adrian Booth. *Children of the Grave.* DVD by Spooked Television Releasing, 2007. Aired on SyFy Channel as documentary, October 2009.

Cassadaga Spiritualist Camp: 2005/2006 Annual Program. Camp office located at 1325 Stevens Street, Cassadaga, FL 32706.

Charon, Jean E. *The Unity of Mind & Matter Part III: The Universe, ARIADNE'S WEB,* Volume 2, Number 1. Dallas: Rayeson Enterprises, Autumn, 1996.

Coelho, Paul. *The Alchemist.* New York: HarperCollins, 2005.

Crescent Hotel & Spa. *Welcome to the Historic 1886 Crescent Hotel & Spa.* Brochure: 2007. Information and photo printed with permission of management.

Davis, Roy Eugene. *A Master Guide to Meditation & Spiritual Growth.* Lakemont: CSA Press, 2002.

Einstein, Albert, Estate of. *Albert Einstein In His Own Words.* New York: Portland House/Random House Value Publishing, 2000.

Enchanted Learning. Definition: Universe. EnchantedLearning.com © 1999-2009. http://www.enchantedlearning.com/subjects/astronomy/glossary/indexu.shtml.

Grimassi, Raven. *Wiccan Magick: Inner Teachings Of The Craft.* St. Paul: Llewellyn Publications, 2000.

Hall, Katie, and John Pickering. *Beyond Photography: Encounters with Orbs, Angels and Mysterious Light-Forms!* Washington: O Books, 2006.

MacLean, Kenneth James Michael. *The Vibrational Universe: Harnessing the Power of Thought to Consciously Create Your Life.* Ann Arbor: Loving Healing Press, 2006.

Merriam-Webster Online Dictionary. Definition: Universe. © 2009, Merriam-Webster, Incorporated. http://www.merriam-webster.com/dictionary/Universe.

Neihardt, John G. *Black Elk Speaks: Being the Life Story of a Holy Man of the Oglala Sioux.* Lincoln: University of Nebraska Press, 1988.

Redfield, James. *The Celestine Prophecy: An Adventure.* New York: Warner Books, 1994.

Reilly, Carmel. *True Tales of Angel Encounters.* Woodbury: Llewellyn Publications, 2009.

Reynolds, David S. *Waking Giant: America in the Age of Jackson*. New York: HarperCollins, 2008.

Robinson, Lynn B., PhD. *Coming Out Of Your Psychic Closet: How To Unlock Your Naturally Intuitive Self.* Mobile: Factor Press, 1994.

Sweet, Leonore, PhD. *How To Photograph The Paranormal.* Charlottesville: Hampton Roads Publishing, 2005.

Teresa, Mother, and Thomas Moore. *No Greater Love.* Novato: New World Library, 2002.

Tolle, Eckhart. *The Power of Now.* Vancouver: Namaste Publishing, 2004.

Van Praagh, James. *Ghosts Among Us: Uncovering the Truth About the Other Side.* New York: HarperCollins, 2008.

Weiss, Brian, MD. *Many Lives, Many Masters.* New York: Fireside/Simon & Schuster, 1988.

Wolf, Fred Alan, PhD. *The Spiritual Universe: One Physicist's Vision of Spirit, Soul, Matter, and Self.* Needham: Moment Point Press, 1999.

Zukav, Gary. *The Seat Of The Soul.* New York: Fireside/Simon & Schuster, 1990.

LaVergne, TN USA
23 March 2011
221269LV00001B/69/P